The COMPLETE COLOUR COOKBOOK

The COMPLETE COLOUR COOKBOOK

INDEX

Published 1994 by Merehurst Limited,
Ferry House, 51-57 Lacy Road, Putney, London SW15 1PR

ISBN 1 85391 389 8

A catalogue record of this book is available from the British Library.

Recipes by Mary Cadogan, Maxine Clark, Moyra Fraser, Carole Handslip, Janice Murfitt, Lyn Rutherford, Mandy Wagstaff

Compiled by Janet Illsley
Designed by Maggie Aldred
Photography by Ken Field, David Gill,
James Murphy, Alan Newnham
Typesetting by BMD Graphics Ltd
Colour separation by Fotographics Ltd, UK–Hong Kong
Printed in Italy by G Canale & C SpA

The material in this book also appears in the following titles in the Merehurst Cookery Series:
Barbecues, Cakes, Children's Parties, Desserts, Light Meals, Party Food, Salads, Soups, Starters, Vegetables

INTRODUCTION

This comprehensive collection of imaginative recipes truly reflects the state of the art of cooking in the nineties. There is an emphasis on the use of fresh ingredients, assembled with carefully chosen flavourings to produce delicious, fresh-tasting dishes. Preparation techniques and cooking methods are deliberately kept simple, to save that valuable commodity – time!

The range of ingredients available on our supermarket shelves and in our markets has never been greater.

Consider the ever-increasing variety of fresh fruit and vegetables; the new leaner, tender cuts of meat and poultry; fresh fish and shellfish; flavouring ingredients, such as extra-virgin olive oil, sun-dried tomatoes, balsamic vinegar... and so on.

The recipes in this collection will help you to make the most of these wonderful ingredients.

Whether you are entertaining in style or simply cooking for family or friends, you will find plenty of inspiration here.

NOTES

Quantities are given in metric, imperial and cup measurements.
Use only one set of measures, because they are not interchangeable.

All spoon measures are level: 1 tablespoon = 15 ml spoon; 1 teaspoon = 5 ml spoon.

Use fresh herbs and freshly ground black pepper unless otherwise stated.

Use size 3 eggs unless otherwise specified.

Ovens and grills must be preheated to the temperature specified in the recipe.

Contents

Soups

Soups for all seasons are included here, from sustaining chunky versions packed with nourishing ingredients to refreshing ice-cool summer soups.

For best results use a good quality stock – preferably homemade. Complement your chosen soup with a tasty flavoured bread or one of the original accompaniment ideas suggested in this chapter.

ROQUEFORT & ALMOND SOUP

Roquefort and almonds marry perfectly in this creamy, smooth-textured soup. However, you could substitute Stilton if you prefer. Cheese profiteroles (right) make an ideal crisp accompaniment.

1 tablespoon sunflower oil · 1 clove garlic, crushed 1 tablespoon flour · 625ml (1 pint/2½ cups) milk 60g (2oz/½ cup) ground almonds · 90g (3 oz) Roquefort cheese, crumbled · 2 tablespoons chopped chervil or parsley · salt and pepper to taste

To Garnish:
chervil or parsley sprigs

1 Heat the oil in a pan, add the garlic and fry gently for 1 minute. Remove from heat and stir in the flour. Stir in 155ml (5fl oz/⅔ cup) of the milk. Stir in the ground almonds. Add remaining milk. Bring to the boil and cook, stirring, for 3 minutes until thickened.
2 Add the Roquefort and chervil or parsley and stir over a gentle heat until the cheese has melted; season.
3 Serve garnished with chervil or parsley. **Serves 6**

CHEESE PROFITEROLES: Sift 5 tablespoons flour with ½ teaspoon mustard and a pinch each of cayenne pepper and salt. Melt 30g (1oz) butter in a pan, add 75ml (2½fl oz/⅓ cup) water and bring to the boil. Add the flour mixture all at once, remove from heat and beat vigorously until the mixture leaves the sides of the pan clean. Gradually beat in 1 beaten egg, then 30g (1oz/¼ cup) finely grated Cheddar cheese, 2 tablespoons Parmesan, and 1 tablespoon toasted sesame seeds.

Using a piping bag fitted with a 5mm (¼ inch) nozzle, pipe small blobs on to a non-stick baking sheet. Bake at 190C (375F/Gas 5) for 15-17 minutes until golden.

SPINACH & GRUYÈRE SOUP

This vibrant soup is delicious served with filo rolls (right). Instead of fresh spinach, defrosted frozen spinach can be used.

2 tablespoons oil · 1 onion, chopped · 2 sticks celery, chopped · 1 tablespoon flour · 470ml (3/4 pint/ 1 1/4 cups) vegetable stock or water · 500g (1lb) spinach · 1/4 teaspoon grated nutmeg · bouquet garni · salt and pepper to taste · 470ml (3/4 pint/ 1 1/4 cups) milk · 2 egg yolks · juice of 1/2 lemon 60g (2oz) gruyère cheese, grated

1 Heat the oil in a saucepan, add the onion and celery and fry until softened. Remove from the heat and stir in the flour, then gradually add the stock or water, stirring until evenly blended. Bring to the boil, stirring.
2 Add the spinach, pressing it down until wilted. Add the nutmeg, bouquet garni and seasoning. Cover and cook gently for 20 minutes. Discard the bouquet garni.
3 Cool slightly, then pour the soup into a food processor or blender and work to a smooth purée. Return to the rinsed-out pan, add the milk and reheat.
4 In a bowl, mix together the egg yolks and lemon juice, then add a ladleful of soup and stir well. Pour back into the soup and cook gently, stirring well until thickened; do not boil or it will curdle. Spoon into individual bowls and sprinkle with the gruyère. **Serves 6**

FILO ROLLS: Mix 90g (3oz) ricotta or feta cheese with 1 tablespoon chopped dill or parsley, adding a little milk to moisten. Cut 6 strips of filo pastry, each 7.5 × 25cm (3 × 10 inches). Brush with melted butter, put a little filling at one end and roll up, folding in ends. Put on a baking sheet, brush with butter and bake at 190C (375F/Gas 5) for 10-15 minutes.

CAULIFLOWER & CRESS SOUP

A delicate smooth soup, especially good served with a cheesy accompaniment, such as cheese sablés (right).

1 bunch watercress · 2 tablespoons oil · 1 onion, chopped · 1 small cauliflower, chopped · 785ml (1 1/4 pints/3 cups) chicken stock · salt and pepper to taste · 4 tablespoons single (light) cream

1 Roughly chop the watercress. Heat the oil in a pan, add the onion and watercress, cover and cook gently for about 10 minutes until softened.

2 Add the cauliflower, stock and seasoning. Bring to the boil, cover and simmer gently for 20 minutes until the cauliflower is cooked.

3 Cool slightly, then pour into a blender or food processor and blend until smooth. Return to the pan and heat through. Pour into warmed individual serving bowls and swirl in the cream. **Serves 6**

CHEESE SABLES: Sift 90g (3oz/3/4 cup) plain flour, 1 teaspoon mustard and a pinch each of cayenne and salt together into a bowl. Rub in 60g (2oz) butter. Add 60g (2oz) grated strong Cheddar cheese and 1 egg yolk; mix to a firm dough. Knead lightly, then roll out thinly on a floured surface to a rectangle, 28 × 15cm (11 × 6 inches). Cut into three 5cm (2 inch) wide strips, brush with egg white and sprinkle with toasted sesame seeds. Cut into 36 small triangles. Chill for 15 minutes. Bake in a preheated oven 190C (375F/Gas 5) for 15 minutes until golden.

PARSNIP & GINGER SOUP

Parsnip and ginger is one of my favourite flavour combinations, but you could substitute carrots for all or some of the parsnip. A flavoursome herb bread makes an ideal accompaniment.

45g (1½oz) butter · 1 onion, chopped
750g (1½lb) parsnips, chopped · 5cm (2 inch) piece fresh root, (green) ginger, finely chopped
875ml (28 fl oz/3½ cups) stock, preferably chicken
2 tablespoons lemon juice · 1 bouquet garni
155ml (5 fl oz/⅔ cup) single (light) cream
salt and pepper to taste

Herb Butter:
60g (2oz) butter, softened · 1 clove garlic, crushed
3 tablespoons chopped herbs, eg parsley, chives, tarragon, chervil, basil, coriander · 1 French stick

To Garnish:
4-6 tablespoons cream

1 Melt the butter in a large pan. Add the onion, parsnips and ginger and sauté gently for 3 minutes, without browning. Add the stock, lemon juice and bouquet garni. Bring to the boil, cover and simmer for 25-30 minutes until the parsnip is tender. Discard the bouquet garni.

2 Meanwhile, make the herb bread. Preheat the oven to 190C (375F/Gas 5). Mix the butter with the garlic and herbs. Slice the French stick and spread the herb butter evenly on the slices. Reassemble the loaf, wrap in foil and bake in the oven for 15 minutes.

3 Purée the soup in a blender or food processor until smooth. Return to the pan and stir in the cream. Reheat gently and season with salt and pepper to taste.

4 Divide the soup between warmed individual soup plates, garnish with swirls of cream and serve immediately, with the herb bread. **Serves 4-6**

TOMATO & PASTA SOUP WITH PESTO

This is a really simple tomato soup enriched with a pungent spoonful of fresh pesto. Serve with warm bread such as ciabatta, the flat Italian loaf flavoured with oil.

750g (1½lb) ripe tomatoes, skinned · 2 celery sticks, chopped · 1 carrot, sliced · 1 small onion, chopped · 1 litre (32 fl oz/4 cups) chicken or vegetable stock · 1 tablespoon tomato purée (paste) · 1 bay leaf · ½ teaspoon sugar · 60g (2oz) small pasta shapes · salt and pepper

Pesto:
30g (1oz) basil leaves, finely chopped 3 tablespoons grated Parmesan cheese · 1 clove garlic, crushed · 30g (1oz) pine nuts, toasted and chopped · 4 tablespoons olive oil

To Garnish:
basil leaves

1 Place the tomatoes, celery, carrot, onion, stock, tomato purée (paste), bay leaf and sugar in a large pan. Bring to the boil and simmer for 30 minutes. Discard the bay leaf and allow to cool slightly.
2 Transfer the soup to a blender or food processor and work to a purée, then return to the pan and bring back to the boil. Add the pasta to the soup and simmer for 10 minutes. Season with salt and pepper to taste.
3 Meanwhile prepare the pesto. Mix all the ingredients together using a pestle and mortar or a wooden spoon and bowl to give a coarse paste.
4 To serve, ladle the soup into warmed individual serving bowls and add a spoonful of pesto to each. Garnish with basil leaves.
Serves 4-6

BLACK BEAN & VEGETABLE SOUP

Cans of preserved black beans are obtainable from Chinese food stores and many supermarkets. They have a superb, but salty, flavour so season this soup with freshly ground pepper only.

60g (2oz) butter · 1 onion, chopped · 125g (4oz) leek, sliced · 2 courgettes (zucchini), sliced 2 carrots, sliced · ½ red pepper, halved, seeded and diced · 315g (10oz) potato, diced · 185g (6oz) French beans, cut into 2.5cm (1 inch) lengths 4 tomatoes, skinned and chopped · 1 litre (32 fl oz/4 cups) vegetable or chicken stock 185g (6oz) frozen shelled broad beans, thawed 4-6 tablespoons preserved black beans, rinsed 2 tablespoons chopped coriander leaves freshly ground black pepper

To Garnish:
coriander or parsley sprigs

1 Melt the butter in a large pan. Add the onion, leek, courgettes (zucchini), carrots, red pepper, potato and French beans and sauté for 3-4 minutes. Add the tomatoes and stock. Bring to the boil, then cover and simmer for 25 minutes.
2 Stir in the broad beans and black beans and continue cooking for 3 minutes.
3 Transfer half the soup to a food processor or blender and work to a fairly smooth purée. Return to the pan, stir in the coriander and reheat gently. Season with freshly ground black pepper to taste.
4 Divide the soup between warmed individual serving bowls and garnish with coriander or parsley. **Serves 6**

Lebanese Lentil Soup

Lentil soup is one of the most popular soups in the Middle East and there are many varieties. I particularly like this sustaining version, which was acquired from a Lebanese friend.

250g (8oz) brown lentils · 2 carrots, chopped 1 potato, chopped · 1.5 litres (2½ pints/6¼ cups) water · salt and pepper to taste · 750g (1½lb) spinach or chard, stalks removed · 4 tablespoons olive oil · 1 onion, chopped · 5 cloves garlic, chopped 1 teaspoon cornflour · juice of 1 lemon 2 tablespoons chopped coriander leaves

1 Put the lentils into a large saucepan with the carrots, potato, water and seasoning. Bring to the boil, cover and simmer gently for 45 minutes.

2 Chop the spinach or chard roughly and add to the saucepan, pressing it down well until it has wilted. Cover and simmer gently for 10 minutes.

3 Heat the oil in a frying pan, add the onions and fry gently for 2-3 minutes until pale golden. Add the garlic and cook for a further 2 minutes, then stir into the soup.

4 Blend the cornflour with the lemon juice and add to the soup with the coriander. Cook, stirring, for a further 2 minutes. Serve piping hot. **Serves 6-8**

MAJORCAN CHICK PEA SOUP

This rustic, peasant soup is perfect for cold wintry days. It should be thick with vegetables and contain very little liquid.

250g (8oz/1 ¼ cups) chick peas, soaked overnight and drained · 3 tablespoons olive oil · 2 leeks, sliced 2 carrots, sliced · 2 sticks celery, sliced · 2 potatoes, chopped · 397g (14oz) can chopped tomatoes 1 bay leaf · 2 cloves garlic, chopped · salt and pepper to taste · ½ small cabbage, shredded 125g (4oz) spinach, shredded

1 Put the chick peas in a saucepan, cover with water, bring to the boil and boil steadily for 10 minutes. Lower the heat, cover and simmer for 45 minutes.

2 Heat the oil in a saucepan, add the leeks, carrots and celery and cook gently for 15 minutes, stirring occasionally.

3 Drain the chick peas, reserving the liquid and make up to 1.25 litres (2 pints/5 cups) with water. Add the liquid to the vegetables with the chick peas, potatoes, tomatoes, bay leaf, garlic and seasoning. Cover and simmer gently for 40 minutes.

4 Add the cabbage and spinach and cook for a further 15 minutes. Discard the bay leaf.

5 Serve piping hot, with crusty bread. **Serves 6**

VARIATION: Replace the chick peas with an alternative pulse, such as haricot beans or black-eyed peas. Soak and cook the beans as above.

AVOCADO & ORANGE SOUP

Citrus juice blends well with avocado and enhances its flavour in this recipe to give a subtle-tasting soup. Caviare-topped melba toasts are the ideal accompaniment.

1 large avocado · 315ml (10 fl oz/1 ¼ cups) milk
315ml (10 fl oz/1 ¼ cups) natural yogurt
½ teaspoon grated onion · ½ teaspoon Worcestershire sauce · salt and pepper to taste
155ml (5 fl oz/⅔ cup) thick sour cream
juice of 1 orange

To Serve:
melba toast (see right) · 1 tablespoon lump fish roe

To Garnish:
few chives

1 Peel the avocado, halve, stone and cut into chunks. Put into a blender or food processor with all the remaining ingredients and blend to a smooth purée. Transfer to a bowl, cover and chill in the refrigerator for 30 minutes.

2 To serve, spoon the soup into individual bowls. Float the melba toasts on top and spoon a little caviare on to each one. Garnish with chives to serve. **Serves 4-6**

MELBA TOASTS: Preheat the oven to 160C (325F/Gas 3); preheat the grill, too. Toast the bread on both sides, cut off the crusts and slice in half horizontally to give wafer-thin slices. Cut diagonally into quarters and place on a baking sheet toasted side down. Bake in the oven for 10 minutes until curled.

GAZPACHO

The ever popular iced soup from Andalusia. Tomatoes ripened in Spain are plump, juicy and full of flavour – this is not always the case with the tomatoes we buy over here. If you can't find really good tomatoes, I suggest you replace half of the water with tomato juice to improve the flavour.

2 slices white bread, crusts removed
625ml (1 pint/2½ cups) cold water · 750g (1½lb) ripe tomatoes, skinned and chopped · ½ small onion, chopped · 2 cloves garlic, crushed
½ cucumber, peeled and chopped · 3 tablespoons olive oil · 2 tablespoons white wine vinegar
salt and pepper to taste

To Serve:
2 slices bread · ½ cucumber, diced · 1 small onion, finely chopped · 1 green pepper, cored, seeded and diced · 1 red pepper, cored, seeded and diced

1 Break the bread into pieces and place in a bowl. Pour half of the water over the bread and leave to soak for 10 minutes.
2 Put the bread and soaking liquid into a blender or food processor with the tomatoes, onion, garlic, cucumber, oil, vinegar and seasoning to taste. Blend until smooth.
3 Pour into a soup tureen and stir in the remaining water. Chill in the refrigerator for about 1 hour.
4 Preheat the oven to 180C (350F/Gas 4). Cut or break the bread into pieces and bake in the oven for 15 minutes to crispen. Put the vegetable accompaniments into small serving dishes.
5 Pour the soup into individual bowls and serve with the crisp bread and accompanying vegetables. **Serves 8**

NOTE: If using tomato juice, as suggested in the introduction, add it to the soup (instead of the water) in step 3.

PRAWN & SWEETCORN SOUP

A popular Cantonese soup which can be made with prawns or white crab meat if you prefer.

785ml (1 ¼ pints/3 cups) chicken stock · 1 teaspoon finely chopped root (green) ginger · 315g (10oz) frozen sweetcorn · salt and pepper to taste · 1 tablespoon cornflour · 1 tablespoon dry sherry · 125g (4oz) peeled prawns · 3 spring onions (green shallots), thinly sliced diagonally · 1 egg · 1 tablespoon sesame oil

1 Put the stock into a large saucepan with the ginger, sweetcorn and seasoning. Bring to the boil, cover and simmer for 10 minutes.
2 Blend the cornflour with the sherry, then add to the soup with the prawns and spring onions (shallots). Cook, stirring, until thickened.
3 In a bowl, whisk the egg and sesame oil together with a fork until well blended. Turn off the heat, then trickle in the egg in a thin stream from the fork, trailing it over the surface in a figure-of-eight movement; do not stir.
4 As soon as the egg sets – within about 30 seconds – ladle the soup into bowls. Serve immediately. **Serves 4**

MUSSEL CHOWDER

A delicious seafood soup, best served with plenty of crusty French bread.

*1kg (2lb) mussels in shells · 60g (2oz) butter
1 onion, chopped · 2 celery sticks, sliced
315g (10oz) potato, diced · 2 cloves garlic, crushed
pinch of saffron strands · 30g (1oz/¼ cup) flour
500ml (16 fl oz/2 cups) fish or vegetable stock
125ml (4 fl oz/½ cup) dry white wine · 1 bouquet garni · 250g (8oz) white fish fillet, eg cod or haddock, skinned and diced · 2 egg yolks
3 tablespoons double (thick) cream · 2 tablespoons chopped parsley · salt and pepper*

To Garnish:
parsley sprigs

1 Scrub the mussels thoroughly, removing the beards and discard any mussels that are open.
2 Melt the butter in a large saucepan. Add the onion, celery, potato, garlic and saffron and cook, stirring, for 3 minutes, without browning. Stir in the flour and continue cooking for 1 minute.
3 Gradually add the stock and wine to the pan, stirring all the time. Bring to the boil, then lower the heat and simmer for 5 minutes. Add the bouquet garni, mussels and fish. Cover and cook for about 6 minutes until the fish is tender and the mussel shells have opened. Discard the bouquet garni and any mussels that remain closed.
4 Blend together the egg yolks and cream. Stir a little hot soup into the mixture then remove the soup from the heat and add the blended mixture and chopped parsley. Stir well and season with salt and pepper to taste. Pour into warmed individual bowls and serve immediately, garnished with parsley. **Serves 6**

VARIATION: Replace the mussels with clams, cleaning and preparing them in the same way.

FISH SOUP WITH SAFFRON

Saffron imparts a warm golden glow to this tasty soup. Served with garlic bread (right), it is a meal in itself. Leeks and fennel blend harmoniously with any white fish, but I normally use a combination of monkfish, halibut and cod.

60g (2oz) butter · 1 large leek, thinly sliced 1 small fennel bulb, thinly sliced lengthways · 315ml (10 fl oz/1¼ cups) white wine · 625ml (1 pint/ 2½ cups) fish stock · 750g (1½lb) white fish, cut into 2.5cm (1 inch) chunks · 3 tomatoes, skinned and roughly chopped · ½ teaspoon powdered saffron · 2 tablespoons chopped parsley 1 tablespoon cornflour · 2 tablespoons water · salt and pepper to taste · ¼ teaspoon tabasco sauce 90ml (3 fl oz/⅓ cup) double (thick) cream

1 Melt the butter in a pan, add the leek and fennel, cover and cook very gently for about 15 minutes, stirring occasionally.

2 Add the wine and fish stock and simmer for 5 minutes. Add the fish chunks, tomatoes, saffron and parsley. Bring to a gentle simmer, cover and cook for 10-12 minutes.

3 Blend the cornflour with the water, add to the soup and stir for 1 minute until thickened. Season with salt, pepper and tabasco and stir in the cream. Serve immediately, with garlic bread if desired. **Serves 4-6**

GARLIC BREAD: Mix 75g (3oz) softened butter with 2 crushed garlic cloves, 1-2 teaspoons chopped parsley if desired, and seasoning to taste. Make diagonal cuts through a French loaf at 2.5cm (1 inch) intervals, almost through to the base. Spread cut surfaces with flavoured butter. Wrap in foil and bake in a preheated oven at 200C (400F/Gas 6) for 15 minutes, loosening the foil for the last 5 minutes to crispen the top.

SOUPE DE POISSONS

The tiny fish used in Mediterranean fish soups are not available here, but a good result can be achieved using fish bones and trimmings, eg, sole, a few unshelled prawns and a little cheap fish. Toasted baguette, spread with rouille and topped with grated cheese, is the classic accompaniment.

2 tablespoons olive oil · 1 onion, sliced · 2 cloves garlic, chopped · 175g (6oz) unshelled prawns 250g (8oz) conger eel, mullet or other cheap white fish · 750g (1½lb) fish bones and trimmings or a head of salmon · 4 tomatoes, quartered 1 tablespoon tomato purée (paste) · bouquet garni 1.5 litres (2½ pints/6¼ cups) water 1 tablespoon white wine vinegar salt and pepper to taste · ¼ teaspoon powdered saffron · 60g (2oz) vermicelli

Rouille:

½ red pepper, cored and seeded · 2 red chillies, seeded · 2 cloves garlic, chopped · 60g (2oz/1 cup) fresh breadcrumbs · 125ml (4 fl oz/½ cup) olive oil

To Serve:

1 baguette, sliced · grated gruyère cheese

1 Heat the oil in a large pan, add the onion, garlic, prawns, fish, fish bones and trimmings, and fry gently until lightly coloured. Add the tomatoes, tomato purée (paste), bouquet garni, water, vinegar and seasoning. Bring to the boil, partially cover and simmer gently for 40 minutes.

2 Meanwhile make the rouille. Grill the red pepper, cut side down, until the skin blackens, then rinse off the black skin. Put into a blender or food processor with the chillies, garlic, breadcrumbs, 2 tablespoons of the fish cooking liquor and seasoning. Blend until smooth, then gradually add the oil through the feeder tube, working until smooth. Transfer to a serving dish.

3 Discard any large pieces of bone, then strain the soup through a sieve, pressing through as much fish as possible to extract the maximum flavour.

4 Return to the rinsed-out saucepan and bring to the boil. Add the saffron and vermicelli and cook for 5 minutes.

5 Serve the soup with the rouille, toasted baguette and grated gruyère cheese.

Serves 6

LOBSTER BISQUE

One of the most delicious of all soups – to be reserved for very special occasions. It is at its best served with croûtons (right) for a contrast in texture.

1 small cooked lobster · 30g (1 oz) butter · 1 tablespoon oil · 1 onion, chopped · 1 carrot, chopped · 90g (3oz/½ cup) rice · 250ml (8 fl oz/1 cup) dry white wine · 1.75 litres (3 pints/7½ cups) fish stock · bouquet garni · 90ml (3 fl oz/⅓ cup) double (thick) cream · 60ml (2 fl oz/¼ cup) brandy · salt and cayenne pepper to taste

1 Lay the lobster on a chopping board with the hard shell uppermost and cut in half lengthwise. Open out the two halves and remove the black intestinal thread which runs down the tail, and the small sac in the head behind the eyes; these are the only parts to discard. The greenish liver should be retained.
2 Remove the tail meat, claw meat and any coral and reserve.
3 Heat the butter and oil in a large saucepan, add the onion and carrot and cook until softened.
4 Add the lobster shells to the pan with the rice, wine, stock and bouquet garni. Cover and cook for 30 minutes.
5 Discard the lobster shells and bouquet garni. Transfer the contents of the saucepan to a blender or food processor, add the claw meat and liver and blend until smooth. Pass the soup through a sieve to obtain a really smooth texture.
6 Mash the coral (if any) and stir into the soup with the cream, brandy and seasoning. Slice the reserved lobster tail meat, add to the soup and reheat gently. Ladle into individual serving bowls and serve immediately. **Serves 6**

CROUTONS: Shallow fry 3mm (¼ inch) cubes of bread in hot oil until golden brown. Drain on absorbent kitchen paper.

COCK-A-LEEKIE

A wonderful soup from Scotland, which sometimes has a few prunes added. Traditionally a capon or boiling fowl is used, as the long slow cooking ensures its tenderness. You can of course use chicken instead.

1 capon, boiling fowl or chicken · 1 onion, quartered
2 carrots, roughly chopped · bouquet garni
6 peppercorns · 1 teaspoon salt · 1.75 litres (3 pints/7½ cups) water · 45g (1½oz) butter
750g (1½lb) leeks, sliced into rings · 2 tablespoons chopped parsley

1 Put the poultry and its giblets into a large saucepan with the onion, carrots, bouquet garni, peppercorns and salt, then add the water. Bring to the boil and skim off any scum that rises to the surface. Cover and simmer gently for 1¼-1½ hours until the poultry is cooked; a boiling fowl will take a little longer.
2 Lift out the poultry. Strain the stock, allow to cool, then refrigerate until the fat becomes solid. Discard the fat.
3 Remove the breast from the bird and reserve for another dish. Remove the skin from the wings and legs and cut the meat into fairly large pieces.
4 Heat the butter in a pan, add the leeks, cover and cook very gently for 10 minutes until softened. Add the stock and seasoning. Bring to the boil, cover and simmer gently for 15 minutes. Add the chicken and parsley, reheat for a few minutes and serve. **Serves 6-8**

RIOJAN POTATO SOUP

A rustic peasant soup from the Rioja area of Spain. Use a good quality chorizo sausage – strong, spicy and full of paprika, so that the flavour will permeate the soup and give it a pinky hue.

2 tablespoons olive oil · 1 large onion, chopped 4 cloves garlic, chopped · 750g (1½lb) potatoes, cut into chunks · 940ml (1½ pints/3 cups) chicken stock · 1 bay leaf · salt and pepper to taste 2 chorizo sausages, about 185g (6oz) total weight, sliced · 2 tablespoons chopped parsley

1 Heat the oil in a pan, add the onion and fry until softened. Add the garlic and potato chunks and cook, turning for 2 minutes until coated in oil.

2 Add the stock, bay leaf and seasoning. Bring to the boil, cover and simmer gently for 30 minutes until the potatoes are well cooked and beginning to break up.

3 Add the chorizo slices and parsley. Cook for a further 5 minutes to heat through. Remove the bay leaf before serving. **Serves 4**

VARIATION: Replace the potatoes with 250g (8oz/1¼ cups) butter beans. Soak them overnight in cold water to cover, then drain and add to the soup with an additional 470ml (¾ pint/2 cups) stock. Cook the soup for 1½ hours, then add the chorizo slices and chopped parsley and cook for 5 minutes.

SPICED LAMB & COCONUT SOUP

Flavours of Malaysia – provided by lemon grass, chilli, coconut and spices – make this an unusual main course soup.

750g (1½lb) neck of lamb · 1 clove garlic, crushed 2 bay leaves · 1 stalk lemon grass · 1 green chilli, halved and seeded · 2 teaspoons coriander seeds, lightly crushed · 1 teaspoon cumin seeds, lightly crushed · 1 teaspoon garam masaia · 1 litre (32 fl oz/4 cups) stock or water · 125g (4oz/⅔ cup) red lentils · 60g (2oz) creamed coconut · 1 onion, chopped · 2 large carrots, grated · 250g (8oz) potato, diced · 2 sticks celery, sliced · 125g (4oz) sweetcorn kernels · salt and pepper

To Garnish:
toasted coconut · coriander or parsley sprigs

1 Trim the lamb and remove the fat. Place in a large pan with the garlic, bay leaves, lemon grass, chilli and spices. Add the stock or water, bring to the boil, then cover and simmer for 1½ hours, skimming occasionally. Discard the bay leaves, lemon grass and chilli.
2 Using a slotted spoon, remove the meat from the pan and set aside. Add the lentils, coconut and vegetables to the pan. Bring to the boil and simmer for 30 minutes, until the lentils and vegetables are tender. Transfer half of the soup to a food processor or blender and work to a purée. Return to the pan.
3 Remove the lamb from the bone, cut into 2.5cm (1 inch) pieces and add to the soup. Reheat and simmer for a further 5 minutes. Season with salt and pepper to taste. Serve hot, sprinkled with toasted coconut and garnished with coriander or parsley. **Serves 6**

CHINESE HOT & SOUR SOUP

This Northern Chinese peasant soup is sharp and spicy with a glutinous consistency. Bean thread noodles – also known as cellophane or transparent noodles – are made from ground mung beans. They are sold in small bundles in oriental food stores.

125g (4oz) lean pork, cut into thin strips · 30g (1 oz) dried mushrooms · 30g (1 oz) bean thread noodles
3 tablespoons rice vinegar · 1 teaspoon sesame oil
2 tablespoons dark soy sauce · 2 teaspoons sugar
1 teaspoon chilli sauce · 1½ tablespoons cornflour
625ml (1 pint/2½ cups) strong chicken stock
315g (10oz) bean curd, drained and cut into 1cm (½ inch) cubes · 1 egg, lightly whisked
4 spring onions (green shallots), sliced diagonally
2 tablespoons coriander leaves, chopped

To Serve:
sesame oil to taste

1 Put the pork into a small pan, cover with boiling water, bring back to the boil and cook for 2 minutes; drain and reserve the liquid.
2 Soak the mushrooms in boiling water to cover for 20 minutes, then drain, adding the soaking liquid to the pork liquid. Discard the mushroom stems and slice the caps.
3 Soak the noodles in hot water to cover for 5 minutes, then drain and cut into 7.5cm (3 inch) lengths.
4 In a bowl, mix together the vinegar, sesame oil, soy sauce, sugar, chilli sauce and cornflour until smooth.
5 Put the chicken stock in a saucepan. Make the pork and mushroom liquid up to 625ml (1 pint/2½ cups) with water if necessary, add to the pan and bring to the boil. Add the pork, mushrooms, noodles and bean curd and simmer for 3 minutes.
6 Stir in the cornflour mixture and simmer, stirring, for 3 minutes until thickened.
7 Turn off the heat, then trickle in the egg from a fork, trailing it over the surface in a figure-of-eight movement; do not stir for about 30 seconds by which time the egg will have set.
8 Gently stir in the spring onions (shallots) and coriander, with sesame oil to taste. **Serves 6**

CHILLI CHICKEN SOUP

A substantial, warming main meal soup of chicken, vegetables and beans flavoured with chilli. It is delicious served with garlic bread or crusty maize bread.

125g (4oz/⅔ cup) red kidney beans · 90g (3oz/½ cup) haricot beans · 60g (2oz) butter · 1 onion, chopped · 2 cloves garlic, crushed · 4 boneless chicken thighs, skinned and chopped · 1 bouquet garni · 625ml (20 fl oz/2½ cups) chicken stock · 397g (14oz) can chopped tomatoes · 1-2 teaspoons chilli powder · 2 tablespoons tomato purée (paste) · 1 tablespoon Worcestershire sauce · 3 sticks celery, sliced · 250g (8oz) turnip or swede, diced · 2 courgettes (zucchini), sliced · 1 tablespoon chopped parsley · salt and pepper

1 Soak the kidney beans and haricot beans in cold water overnight. Drain.

2 Put the soaked beans in a large pan, cover with water and bring to the boil. Boil steadily for 10 minutes, then lower the heat, cover and simmer for 1 hour; top up with more boiling water as necessary. Drain and set aside.

3 Melt the butter in a large pan. Add the onion, garlic and chicken and sauté for 5 minutes. Add the bouquet garni, stock, tomatoes, chilli powder, tomato purée (paste), Worcester sauce, and vegetables. Stir well and bring to the boil. Cover and simmer for 25 minutes, until the vegetables are tender.

4 Discard the bouquet garni. Stir the parsley and beans into the soup, reheat and season with salt and pepper to taste. Serve hot.

Serves 6

VARIATION: Replace the turnip with diced carrots and flavour the soup with 1 tablespoon chopped fresh coriander instead of parsley.

STARTERS

A superb collection of stylish starters to suit all types of menus. Choose from crisp, colourful salads, mouth-watering grilled and baked vegetables, delicate seafood starters and more substantial meat dishes. Remember to select a recipe which contrasts and complements the rest of the meal to follow.

TRICOLORE SALAD

The simplest of all salads, and a perfect starter. Use as much fresh basil as you can afford. If you cannot find cocktail avocados, use a large, sliced avocado instead.

6 ripe tomatoes, sliced · 250g (8oz) mozzarella cheese, sliced · 12 cocktail avocados, peeled and halved · 15-20 basil leaves

Dressing:

6 tablespoons olive oil · 2 tablespoons wine vinegar
1 teaspoon wholegrain mustard · pinch of sugar
salt and pepper to taste

1 Arrange the tomato and mozzarella slices in circles on individual plates. Pile the avocados in the middle and scatter basil leaves over the top.

2 Whisk the dressing ingredients together in a bowl and pour over the salad. Serve immediately. **Serves 4**

CRUDITÉS WITH GARLIC DIP

I first tasted crudités on my very first French holiday in Provençe – truly one of discovery! Eaten with crisp vegetables, it tasted wonderful.

Selection of the following:
2 red or yellow peppers · 12 radishes
12 baby carrots · ½ cucumber · 125g (4oz) small mange tout (snow peas) or sugar snap peas
12 baby corn · 2 sticks celery · 12 quail's eggs

Aioli:
8 tablespoons good quality mayonnaise
2-3 cloves garlic, crushed · salt and pepper to taste

To Garnish:
herb sprigs

1 First prepare the aioli. In a bowl, mix the mayonnaise with the garlic and seasoning.
2 Halve and seed the peppers and cut into long wedges. Trim the radishes, leaving a little greenery on the ends. Peel and trim the carrots. Halve the cucumber lengthwise, scoop out the seeds and cut the flesh into sticks. Blanch the mange tout (snow peas) or sugar snaps, and baby corn in boiling water for 1 minute; refresh in cold water and drain. Trim celery and cut into sticks.
3 Place the quail's eggs in a saucepan containing cold water to cover and bring to the boil. Boil for 2 minutes, then plunge the eggs into cold water to cool. Partially peel the eggs.
4 Arrange the vegetables and eggs on a large platter or individual serving plates. Cover and chill until required. Garnish with herbs and serve with aioli. **Serves 4**

QUAIL'S EGGS IN ASPARAGUS NEST

This attractive starter features delicate quail's eggs nestling in a bed of fine asparagus tossed with slivers of ham.

12 fresh quail's eggs · 500g (1lb) sprue asparagus
salt and pepper to taste · 1 slice ham, cut into strips
125g (4oz) unsalted butter, melted

1 Place the quail's eggs in a shallow pan and cover with cold water. Bring to the boil and boil for 1 minute. Drain, cover with cold water and partially peel when cool enough to handle.

2 Trim the asparagus, cut into 5cm (2 inch) lengths and cook in boiling salted water for 2 minutes; drain.

3 Toss the asparagus with the ham and arrange in 'nests' on warmed individual plates. Place 3 quail's eggs in each nest. Top with melted butter and seasoning to serve.

Serves 4

TURKISH AUBERGINES (EGGPLANTS)

Also known as 'Imam Bayaldi', meaning 'the priest fainted'. As legend has it, the Imam collapsed when he tasted the delights of this dish! Be lavish with the olive oil – it makes all the difference.

4 small or 2 large aubergines (eggplants) · salt and pepper to taste · 250ml (8 fl oz/1 cup) olive oil 2 large onions, thinly sliced · 3 cloves garlic, crushed 500g (1 lb) tomatoes, skinned, or 440g (14oz) can chopped tomatoes, drained · 4 tablespoons chopped coriander leaves · ½ teaspoon ground cinnamon 1 teaspoon sugar · juice of ½ lemon

To Garnish:

chopped coriander or parsley and extra sprigs

1 Halve the aubergines (eggplants), scoop out the flesh, chop roughly and reserve, leaving 1cm (½ inch) thick shells. Sprinkle the shells with salt and place upside down on a board. Leave for 30 minutes to disgorge the bitter juices.

2 Heat 4 tablespoons olive oil in a saucepan, add the onions and cook gently for 10 minutes until soft but not browned. Add the garlic and cook for a further 2 minutes.

3 If using fresh tomatoes, halve them and squeeze out the seeds. Add the tomatoes to the onions with the coriander, cinnamon, chopped aubergine (eggplant), salt and pepper.

4 Preheat the oven to 150C (300F/Gas 2). Rinse the aubergines (eggplant) shells and pat dry with absorbent kitchen paper. Place, close together, in an ovenproof dish and spoon in the filling. Mix the remaining olive oil, sugar and lemon juice with 155ml (5 fl oz/⅔ cup) water and pour over and around the aubergines (eggplants). Cover and bake in the oven for 1 hour or until very soft. Cool, then chill for about 30 minutes.

5 Sprinkle with plenty of chopped coriander or parsley and garnish with extra sprigs to serve. **Serves 4**

STUFFED MUSHROOMS

Sun-dried tomatoes with their concentrated caramelized tomato flavour make an excellent filling for stuffed mushrooms. They can be bought in large supermarkets and Italian delicatessens – dried or preserved in oil; use the latter here.

8 large cup mushrooms · 6 tablespoons olive oil
2 rashers streaky bacon, rinds removed, chopped
4 shallots, finely chopped · 8-12 sun-dried tomatoes in oil, drained and roughly chopped · 2 tablespoons white wine · 2 tablespoons balsamic or wine vinegar salt and pepper to taste · 2 tablespoons chopped parsley

To Garnish:
parsley sprigs

1 Preheat the oven to 200C (400F/Gas 6). Remove the stalks from the mushrooms, roughly chop them and reserve.

2 Heat half of the oil in a frying pan, add the bacon and fry until golden. Add the shallots and cook over a gentle heat for 5 minutes until soft. Add the sun-dried tomatoes, wine, vinegar and chopped mushroom stalks. Cook for 2-3 minutes until reduced. Add seasoning.

3 Place the mushrooms, cup side up, on a baking sheet and spoon in the filling. Drizzle with the remaining olive oil and bake in the oven for 10 minutes. Transfer the mushrooms to individual serving plates and sprinkle with chopped parsley. Garnish with parsley sprigs and serve immediately.

Serves 4

WILD MUSHROOM FILO TARTLETS

Tartlets as light as air filled with wild mushrooms if you have the courage to pick them! I have found wonderful chanterelles in a forest in my native Scotland – a magical find! A mixture of shitake, oyster and flat mushrooms would do just as well.

2-3 sheets frozen filo pastry, thawed
125g (4oz) butter, melted · 1 clove garlic, crushed
2 shallots, finely chopped · 375g (12oz) mixed mushrooms, wiped and roughly chopped
4 tablespoons white wine · salt and pepper to taste

To Garnish:
herb sprigs

1 Preheat the oven to 200C (400F/Gas 6). Cut the filo pastry into twelve 10cm (4 inch) squares and brush liberally with melted butter. Lay a square in each of 4 individual 7.5cm (3 inch) flan tins. Cover each of these with another filo square, moving the tins a quarter-turn round. Repeat with remaining squares carefully frilling the edges and points, while retaining a good hollow in each centre. Bake in the oven for 8-10 minutes, until crisp and golden. Keep warm.

2 Heat the remaining butter in a frying pan, add the garlic and shallots and fry gently for 5 minutes until just turning golden. Add the mushrooms and white wine. Cook over a high heat for 2 minutes. Add seasoning.

3 Spoon the filling into the filo cases and garnish with herb sprigs. Serve immediately. **Serves 4**

GRILLED CHICORY WITH FETA

Grilling chicory transforms its bitter flavour to delicious effect. Here it is complemented by slices of pear, crumbled feta and thyme.

4 heads of chicory (witlof) · olive oil for basting
1 large ripe pear, cored and sliced · 250g (8oz) feta cheese, crumbled · 1-2 teaspoons chopped thyme
freshly ground black pepper

1 Preheat the grill to high. Cut the chicory (witlof) in half lengthways and brush with oil. Place in the grill pan, cut side up, and grill (as near to the heat as possible) for 3-4 minutes, until just beginning to char and soften. Turn, baste with more oil and cook for a further 2-3 minutes.
2 Carefully turn again and top with pear slices. Brush with oil and grill for 1 minute. Sprinkle the feta and thyme on top and season with pepper. Grill until the cheese is brown and bubbling; the chicory should be very soft. Carefully transfer to warmed individual plates and serve at once.

Serves 4

ASPARAGUS MIMOSA

An ideal starter to serve during late spring, when homegrown asparagus is at its best.

2 hard-boiled eggs, halved · 90g (3oz) butter, softened · 155ml (5 fl oz/⅔ cup) thick sour cream salt and pepper to taste · 2 tablespoons chopped chervil or parsley · 500g (1lb) asparagus 2 tablespoons lemon juice

1 Sieve the egg yolks and finely chop the whites. In a bowl, beat half of the yolks into the butter, then gradually beat in the sour cream. Season and stir in half of the herbs.

2 Trim off the woody ends from the asparagus, making sure they are all the same length. Bring a large, wide pan of water to the boil and add the lemon juice and a good pinch of salt. Add the asparagus and simmer for 10-15 minutes, depending on thickness, until tender; the asparagus should just yield when pierced with the tip of a sharp knife; drain thoroughly.

3 Arrange on individual serving plates, sprinkle with the remaining egg and herbs and serve with the dipping sauce. **Serves 4**

ROQUEFORT & HAZELNUT SOUFFLÉ

Don't be frightened by soufflés! They are easy to make and can be kept uncooked in the fridge until 15 minutes before serving – let your guests wait – the drama makes it all the more exciting!

45g (1½oz) butter · 30g (1oz/¼ cup) plain flour
315ml (10 fl oz/1¼ cups) milk · 155g (5oz) Roquefort, crumbled · 4 eggs, separated
125g (4oz/¾ cup) shelled hazelnuts, toasted and chopped · salt and pepper to taste
1 tablespoon chopped dill

To Garnish:
dill sprigs

1 Preheat the oven to 190C (375F/Gas 5). Lightly grease 4 to 6 ramekins with butter.
2 Melt the butter in a small saucepan, add the flour and cook, stirring, for 1 minute. Remove from the heat and quickly pour in the milk, whisking constantly. Return to the heat and bring to the boil, whisking all the time to avoid lumps.
3 Stir in the Roquefort, egg yolks, three-quarters of the hazelnuts, salt, pepper and chopped dill.
4 In a large bowl, whisk the egg whites with a pinch of salt until stiff. Stir a spoonful of the whisked egg whites into the cheese mixture, then carefully fold in the rest. Spoon into the ramekins and level the tops with a knife. Sprinkle with the remaining hazelnuts.
5 Bake in the oven for 15-20 minutes or until well risen and brown on top. Serve immediately, garnished with dill sprigs.

Serves 4-6

VARIATION: Use another creamy soft blue cheese – such as St. Agur – in place of the Roquefort.

THREE CHEESE TARTLETS

The mozzarella in these savoury tartlets melts to give delicious pockets of molten cheese; the accompanying tomato salsa cuts through the richness.

250g (8oz) packet frozen shortcrust pastry, thawed
185g (6oz/¾ cup) fromage frais · 2 eggs, beaten
60g (2oz) Parmesan cheese, freshly grated
salt and pepper to taste · grated nutmeg to taste
220g (7oz) mozzarella cheese

Tomato Salsa:
2 large beef or plum tomatoes, skinned
8 basil leaves, shredded · 2-3 teaspoons olive oil

To Garnish:
basil sprigs

1 Preheat the oven to 190C (375F/Gas 5). Roll out the pastry very thinly on a floured surface. Cut out four 15cm (6 inch) circles and use to line 7.5cm (3 inch) fluted flan tins. Trim off excess pastry. Line with greaseproof paper discs and baking beans and bake blind for 10 minutes. Remove paper and beans and bake for a further 5 minutes.

2 In a bowl, mix the fromage frais with the eggs and half of the Parmesan. Season with salt, pepper and nutmeg.

3 Cut the mozzarella into 1cm (½ inch) cubes and divide equally between the pastry cases. Pour in the egg and cheese mixture and sprinkle with the remaining Parmesan. Bake for 15-20 minutes until firm and golden brown.

4 Meanwhile, make the tomato salsa. Halve the tomatoes and discard the seeds. Roughly chop the flesh and mix with the basil, olive oil, salt and pepper.

5 Place each tartlet on a warmed serving plate and add a generous spoonful of tomato salsa. Garnish with basil and serve immediately.

Serves 4

NOTE: These tartlets must be freshly made or you won't have lovely pockets of melted cheese in the middle!

SMOKED SALMON BUNDLES

This simple starter can be rustled up very quickly. Filo pastry freezes well, so it's always worth keeping a packet in the freezer.

3 sheets filo pastry, thawed if frozen
melted butter for brushing

Filling:
185g (6oz) smoked salmon, diced · 375g (12oz) ricotta or curd cheese · 2 tablespoons chopped chives or dill · pinch of ground nutmeg salt and pepper to taste

Dill Butter Sauce:
1 shallot, finely chopped · 3 tablespoons (9 tsp) white wine vinegar · 3 tablespoons water 250g (8oz) unsalted butter, chilled and cubed squeeze of lemon juice · 2 tablespoons chopped dill or fennel

To Garnish:
dill or fennel sprigs

1 Preheat the oven to 200C (400F/Gas 6). To make the filling, in a bowl mix together the salmon, ricotta or curd cheese, chives or dill, nutmeg and seasoning, until smooth.
2 Cut the filo pastry into twelve to sixteen 10cm (4 inch) squares. Brush with melted butter and place a spoonful of salmon filling in the middle of each square. Draw the pastry up around the filling, pinching to form a money-bag shape. Spread the frilly tops decoratively.
3 Place on a greased baking sheet and brush with melted butter. Bake in the oven for 10-15 minutes until golden brown.
4 Meanwhile make the dill butter sauce. Put the shallot, vinegar and water in a small pan. Bring to the boil and boil steadily until reduced to 2 tablespoons. Over a low heat, gradually whisk in the butter, a piece at a time, until creamy and amalgamated; this process shouldn't take too long. Do not allow to boil or the sauce will separate. Stir in the dill or fennel and seasoning.
5 Arrange the smoked salmon bundles on warmed individual serving plates and tie a herb sprig around each one to garnish. Spoon a little sauce around the bundles and serve immediately. **Serves 4**

BLINIS

A Russian favourite of mine: yeasty pancakes made with buckwheat and plain flour; topped with thick sour cream and caviare or lumpfish roe. Chopped hard-boiled egg and onion are also popular accompaniments. I like to serve tiny blinis with drinks as canapés.

125g (4oz/1 cup) buckwheat or wholemeal flour
1 tablespoon easy-blend yeast · 1 teaspoon sugar
375ml (12 fl oz/1 ½ cups) warm milk
125g (4oz/1 cup) plain flour · pinch of salt · 2 eggs
1 tablespoon melted butter · oil or lard for frying
butter for spreading

Toppings:
thick sour cream · lumpfish roe or caviare · smoked salmon · pickled herring · chopped hard-boiled egg chopped onion

1 In a large bowl, mix the buckwheat or wholemeal flour with the easy-blend yeast and sugar. Gradually beat in half of the warm milk.

2 Sift the plain flour and salt into another bowl. Make a well in the centre and add 1 whole egg, plus 1 yolk. Add the remaining milk and melted butter. Beat well to form a smooth batter, then beat into the yeast mixture. Cover the bowl with plastic wrap and leave to rise in a warm place for 1-2 hours.

3 Whisk the reserved egg white and fold into the batter. Preheat a heavy pan or griddle and grease with oil or lard. Drop tablespoons of the batter on to the griddle or pan, spacing them well apart. Turn over when bubbles appear on the surface and cook until just turning brown.

4 Spread immediately with a little butter, wrap in foil and keep warm in a preheated cool oven. Put the toppings into serving bowls and allow everyone to add their choice to the blinis. **Serves 4**

SMOKED SALMON PARCELS

Smoked salmon bundles, tied up with chives and served with simply dressed salad leaves and toast triangles, make a pretty and elegant starter.

2 eggs, hard boiled · 125g (4oz) cream cheese
3 tablespoons double (thick) cream · 2 teaspoons snipped chives · salt and pepper to taste · 4 slices smoked salmon · few whole chives · about 125g (4oz) mixed salad leaves, such as chicory (witlof), red cos lettuce, frisée (endive), watercress, lamb's lettuce (corn salad)

Dressing:
4 tablespoons olive oil · 2 tablespoons lemon juice
1/4 teaspoon Dijon mustard · pinch of sugar

1 Finely chop the hard-boiled eggs. Place in a bowl with the cream cheese, cream and chives and mix well. Season with salt and pepper.
2 Lay the smoked salmon slices flat and divide the cream cheese mixture between them. Roll or fold to enclose the filling. Tie each 'parcel' with whole chives to garnish and refrigerate, covered with plastic wrap. until required.
3 To make the dressing, stir all the ingredients in a small bowl or shake in a screw-top jar until combined. Season with salt and pepper to taste.
4 Just before serving put the salad leaves into a bowl, add the dressing and toss gently to mix. Arrange the salad leaves on individual serving plates with the salmon parcels. Serve with wholewheat toast. **Serves 4**

WARM SCALLOP & BACON SALAD

Otherwise known as a 'salade tiede' or warm salad, this is always popular. Use any combination of mixed bitter salad leaves. Make sure everyone has a napkin in case the dressing splashes!

6 fresh scallops · 3 tablespoons olive oil
125g (4oz) pancetta or streaky bacon, derinded and sliced · ½ small frisée (curly endive) · handful of lamb's lettuce (corn salad) · few radicchio leaves and/or oak leaf lettuce

Dressing:
6 tablespoons olive oil · 2 tablespoons sherry or wine vinegar · 2 cloves garlic, finely chopped · 1 teaspoon Dijon mustard · salt and pepper to taste
2 tablespoons double (thick) cream (optional)

To Garnish:
parsley sprigs

1 To make the dressing, whisk together the oil, vinegar, garlic, mustard and seasoning in a small saucepan, until thickened. Heat gently and keep warm.

2 Remove the tough muscle opposite the coral on each scallop. Separate the coral and cut the scallops in half horizontally. Lightly score each scallop disc in a lattice pattern with a sharp knife.

3 Heat the oil in a frying pan, add the bacon and fry over a high heat until brown and crisp. Add the scallops, including the coral, and stir-fry for 2-3 minutes until just opaque.

4 Arrange the salad leaves on individual serving plates. Top with the bacon and scallop mixture. Whisk the cream into the warm dressing, pour over the salad and serve immediately, garnished with parsley. **Serves 4**

PRAWNS IN 'SEAWEED' NESTS

Chinese crispy 'seaweed' is not seaweed at all but spring greens! This recipe is authentic, easy to make and an excellent starter.

12 large (king) prawns · melted butter for brushing

Seaweed:

375g (12oz) spring greens or cabbage leaves
oil for frying · 1 teaspoon salt
1 teaspoon caster sugar

To Garnish:

toasted almonds or pine nuts

1 First, prepare the 'seaweed'. Remove the thick stalks from the spring greens or cabbage. Roll each leaf tightly from the bottom and slice as finely as possible, using a very sharp knife.

2 Pour oil into a large saucepan to a depth of 5cm (2 inches). Heat the oil to 200C (400F) or until a cube of bread browns in 30 seconds. Add half of the spring greens and fry for about 1 minute until crisp but still retaining their colour. Immediately remove and drain on absorbent kitchen paper. Fry the remaining spring greens or cabbage in the same way. Drain and sprinkle with the salt and sugar.

3 Preheat the grill to high. Pull the legs and head off each prawn. With a sharp knife, make a shallow incision along the back of each prawn to expose the black intestinal vein, then remove it. Rinse prawns under cold water and pat dry.

4 Brush each prawn with melted butter and place on the grill rack. Grill for about 2 minutes on each side or until pink and firm.

5 Make a 'nest' of 'seaweed' on each of 4 individual serving plates. Place 3 prawns in the centre of each nest and scatter with toasted nuts. Pour over any remaining melted butter, if desired. Serve immediately. **Serves 4**

STRIPED FISH TERRINE

The secret of making a light fish mousseline is to chill all the ingredients thoroughly beforehand.

375g (12oz) boned salmon, skinned · 1 egg white
155ml (5 fl oz/⅔ cup) double (thick) cream
lemon juice to taste · salt and pepper to taste
375g (12oz) sole fillets, skinned · 2 tablespoons chopped dill · 1 tablespoon chopped tarragon or parsley · butter for greasing

To Finish:
mustard and cress · crème fraîche

1 Cut the salmon into 2.5cm (1 inch) pieces, place in a blender or food processor and purée until smooth. Add the egg white and blend again until evenly mixed. Place in the refrigerator and chill for at least 30 minutes.

2 Return to the blender or food processor and add the cream, lemon juice and seasoning. Blend until smooth. Chill for 30 minutes.

3 Cut the sole fillets into long strips and roll in the chopped herbs until well coated.

4 Preheat the oven to 180C (350F/Gas 4). Grease a 625ml (20 fl oz/2½ cup) loaf tin or terrine with butter. Spoon one third of the salmon mixture into the tin and spread evenly. Lay the herbed sole strips on top, leaving a border at each side. Carefully spoon the remaining salmon mixture over the sole. Spread evenly and level the surface.

5 Cover with buttered foil and place in a roasting tin, containing enough hot water to come half-way up the sides of the terrine. Bake in the oven for 35 minutes or until a skewer inserted into the centre comes out clean.

6 Lift the terrine out of the roasting tin and leave until cold. Remove the foil, cover with oiled greaseproof paper and weight down. Chill for at least 4 hours before carefully turning out. Cut into slices, arrange on serving plates and garnish with mustard and cress. Serve with crème fraîche.

Serves 4-6

PORK SATAY WITH CUCUMBER SALAD

A Malaysian friend showed me how to make this crunchy cucumber salad when we were preparing the food for an Oriental/English wedding. It goes perfectly with pork satay.

Satay:
500g (1 lb) pork fillet · 1 tablespoon dark soy sauce 2 teaspoons light soy sauce · 2 tablespoons crunchy peanut butter · 1 cm (½ inch) piece fresh root (green) ginger, finely chopped

Cucumber Salad:
½ cucumber, peeled · salt · 1 tablespoon caster sugar · 60ml (2 fl oz/¼ cup) cider vinegar or rice wine vinegar · 1 teaspoon sesame seeds 1 tablespoon sesame oil

To Garnish:
spring onion (shallot) brushes

1 Cut the pork into 2cm (¾ inch) cubes and place in a bowl. Put the remaining satay ingredients in a small bowl and whisk together. Pour over the pork and stir until well coated. Cover and leave to marinate in a cool place for at least 30 minutes or overnight.
2 To prepare the salad, halve the cucumber lengthways and scoop out the seeds with a teaspoon. Cut the cucumber into 2.5 × 1 cm (1 × ½ inch) pieces and place in a colander. Sprinkle liberally with salt and leave for 30 minutes.
3 Rinse the cucumber under cold water and pat dry with absorbent kitchen paper. Mix the remaining salad ingredients together in a bowl, add the cucumber and turn until well coated. Cover and chill in the refrigerator until needed.
4 When ready to serve, preheat the grill to high. Thread the pork on to small (pre-soaked) bamboo skewers and grill for 3-4 minutes on each side, basting frequently. Serve immediately, garnished with spring onion (shallot) brushes and accompanied by the cucumber salad. **Serves 4**

SPRING ONION (SHALLOT) BRUSHES: Feather the leafy ends with a knife and place in a bowl of iced water to open.

CHICKEN & WATER CHESTNUT KEBABS

These little kebabs are very quick to make. Pancetta is a type of Italian streaky bacon and can be bought in a piece to cut into any size. Alternatively, use ordinary streaky bacon and form into little rolls before skewering.

3 large skinned boneless chicken breasts
2 tablespoons light soy sauce · 2cm (¾ inch) piece fresh root (green) ginger, sliced · 1 clove garlic, crushed · 250g (8oz) pancetta or streaky bacon
300g (10oz) can water chestnuts (about 24 chestnuts), drained

To Garnish:
salad leaves

1 Preheat the grill to high. Cut the chicken into 2cm (¾ inch) cubes and place in a shallow dish. Add the soy sauce, ginger and garlic and toss well. Cover and leave to marinate in a cool place for at least 15 minutes.

2 Remove rind from the pancetta or bacon and cut into forty-eight 2cm (¾ inch) squares, 5mm (¼ inch) thick.

3 Drain the chicken, reserving the marinade. Thread the chicken, pancetta and chestnuts alternately on to 12 small bamboo skewers.

4 Cook under the preheated grill for about 4 minutes per side or until the kebabs are crisp and tender, basting frequently with the marinade. Serve immediately, on a bed of salad leaves.

Serves 6

NOTE: To prevent them burning during grilling, pre-soak the bamboo skewers in cold water before use.

CHICKEN LIVER MOUSSE

Rich and creamy, this is my version of an old favourite. Do try to use Marsala, a soft and pungent fortified wine from Sicily – it imparts a warm, almost nutty flavour.

375g (12oz) chicken livers · salt and pepper to taste
1 tablespoon Marsala or brandy · 1 tablespoon olive oil · 250g (8oz) butter, softened · 125ml (4 fl oz/ ½ cup) double (thick) or whipping cream
125ml (4 fl oz/½ cup) clarified butter
8 sage leaves

To Garnish:
salad leaves

1 Pick over the chicken livers; cut out and discard any bitter 'green' bits and any fatty 'strings'. Rinse under cold water and pat dry with absorbent kitchen paper.
2 Sprinkle the livers with a little salt and pepper. Place in a shallow dish with the Marsala or brandy and olive oil. Cover and marinate in a cool place for 1-2 hours.
3 Place a non-stick frying pan over a low heat and add the livers with the marinade. Cook very gently for 10-12 minutes or until they are firm but still pink in the middle when pierced with a sharp knife; the livers should not brown. Allow to cool slightly.
4 Purée the livers in a blender or food processor, gradually adding the butter, until smooth. Add the cream and blend for 2-3 seconds. Check the seasoning.
5 Spoon the mousse into individual pots, smooth the surface and cover each with a thin layer of clarified butter and a couple of sage leaves. Allow to set. Serve garnished with salad leaves and accompanied by hot toast or crisp melba toast. **Serves 4**

TO CLARIFY BUTTER: Cut into cubes and melt slowly in a heavy saucepan over a low heat; do not allow to boil. Carefully spoon off the clear butter, leaving the milky sediment behind.

CHICKEN LIVERS WITH POLENTA

Polenta is made from cornmeal and usually takes ages to cook, but 5-minute versions can be found in Italian delicatessens. So can excellent balsamic vinegar, with its rich sweet sour taste – acquired during ageing in wooden barrels.

1 packet quick-cook polenta mix · 250g (8oz) chicken livers · 2 tablespoons olive oil 2 tablespoons balsamic or sherry vinegar 1 tablespoon chopped sage · salt and pepper to taste · 30g (1oz) butter, melted

To Garnish:
sage sprigs

1 Make up the polenta according to packet directions. Pour into a deep bowl and leave in a cool place for 30 minutes to set.
2 Pick over the chicken livers; cut out and discard any bitter 'green' bits and any fatty 'strings'. Rinse under cold water and pat dry with absorbent kitchen paper.
3 Heat the oil in a non-stick frying pan until hot but not smoking. Add the chicken livers and stir-fry over high heat for about 2 minutes until well browned. Transfer to a plate, using a slotted spoon, and set aside.
4 Preheat the grill to high. Add the vinegar to the juices in the pan and allow to bubble over a gentle heat for 1 minute, scraping up any sediment from the bottom of the pan. Drain the chicken livers, add to the pan and stir-fry for a further 4-5 minutes until firm and just pink inside. Stir in the sage and seasoning. Keep warm.
5 Meanwhile, turn out the polenta and cut into 8 pieces. Brush with melted butter and grill for 1 minute on each side or until browned. Place on individual plates and top with the chicken livers. Garnish with sage and serve immediately. **Serves 4**

VARIATION: Use thickly sliced French bread as a base for the chicken livers in place of the polenta slices.

BRESAOLA WITH PEAR & GORGONZOLA

This starter will appeal to anyone who is crazy about Italian food! The eye-catching salad of air-dried beef, luscious pears and creamy gorgonzola is totally indulgent.

185-250g (6-8oz) gorgonzola cheese · 4-8 slices bresaola · 2 ripe pears · olive oil for drizzling freshly ground black pepper

To Garnish:
black olives

1 Crumble the gorgonzola and divide equally between the slices of bresaola. Roll up or fold over and set aside.
2 Halve and core the pears. Slice finely and arrange on individual serving plates with the bresaola. Drizzle with a little olive oil and sprinkle with pepper. Garnish with black olives to serve. **Serves 4**

PROSCIUTTO WITH EXOTIC FRUITS

A most attractive and refreshing starter which can be varied according to the fruits available.

8 lychees · 1 mango · 1 paw paw (papaya)
1 sharon fruit · 2 kiwi fruit · 8 slices prosciutto (Parma ham) · freshly ground black pepper

1 Partially peel the lychees. Peel and slice the mango, discarding the stone. Peel and halve the pawpaw, scoop out the black seeds and cut the flesh into cubes. Slice the sharon fruit into rounds. Peel and slice the kiwi fruit.
2 Arrange the prosciutto and fruits on individual plates. Sprinkle with black pepper.

Serves 4

SALADS

Make the most of the wonderful variety of salad ingredients now on sale all-year-round with these inspiring recipes. Tasty main course seafood, meat and vegetarian salads are followed by mouth-watering side salads for all seasons. Remember to use good quality oil and vinegar in dressings to ensure success.

SMOKED HADDOCK & RICE SALAD

This salad is based on my own favourite kedgeree recipe and includes lots of whole spices for extra flavour.

185g (6oz) long-grain rice, cooked · 3 eggs, hard-boiled and chopped · 2 tomatoes, skinned and chopped · 2 tablespoons snipped chives · 500g (1lb) smoked haddock fillet · 1 onion, chopped · 1 bay leaf · 1 tablespoon coriander seeds, lightly crushed 1 teaspoon cumin seeds, lightly crushed 315ml (10 fl oz/1 ¼ cups) milk

Dressing:

1 clove garlic, crushed · 3 tablespoons mayonnaise pepper to taste

To Garnish:

lemon slices · few chives

1 Put the rice, chopped eggs, tomatoes and chives in a large salad bowl and set aside.

2 Put the smoked haddock, onion, bay leaf, crushed coriander and cumin seeds in a large frying pan, pour in the milk and bring to the boil. Immediately lower the heat until the liquid is barely simmering and cook for 8-10 minutes, until the fish flakes easily and is cooked through. Using a slotted spoon transfer the fish to a plate and allow to cool. Remove skin and flake the flesh. Add the fish to the salad.

3 To make the dressing, discard the bay leaf from the cooking liquid. Add the garlic and cook over a high heat for 1-2 minutes to reduce by half. Remove from the heat and add the mayonnaise, blending well until smooth. Allow to cool.

4 To serve, add the dressing to the salad and toss lightly to mix. Season with pepper and garnish with lemon slices and chives. **Serves 4**

THAI-STYLE PRAWN SALAD

Oriental foods provide a splendid variety of colours and textures, as well as enticing flavours. In this Thai-style salad the flavour of the prawns is enhanced by the unusual prawn dressing. You can buy jars of prawn paste from specialist oriental food shops.

90g (3oz) mange tout (snow peas) · ½ red pepper, cut into matchsticks · 12 cooked king prawns, peeled · 250g (8oz) can water chestnuts, drained and sliced · 3 spring onions (green shallots), sliced handful of coriander leaves, roughly torn

Dressing:

juice of 2 limes · 1 tablespoon prawn paste 1 tablespoon groundnut or safflower oil · ½ clove garlic, crushed · 2.5 cm (1 inch) piece fresh root (green) ginger, grated · pinch of caster sugar salt and pepper to taste

1 First make the dressing: stir all the ingredients together in a small bowl or shake in a screw-top jar until combined. Set aside.

2 Top and tail the mange tout (snow peas). Blanch in boiling water, together with the red pepper, for about 30 seconds. Rinse and drain well. Transfer to a serving bowl and add the prawns, water chestnuts, spring onions (shallots) and coriander.

3 Pour the prepared dressing over the salad and toss lightly to mix. Serve immediately. **Serves 4**

VARIATION: If you prefer use a variety of cooked seafood, such as squid, mussels, crab claws and scallops. This is a particularly good idea if you need a larger quantity of salad to serve more people.

SALADE TIÈDE

A wonderful salad when you want to serve something quick and easy, but also rather special. Everything can be prepared early in the day, before the sun tempts you into the garden. Only the croûtons, bacon and mushrooms need to be cooked just before you're ready to eat. Serve with plenty of warm baguettes.

½ frisée (curly endive) · 1 oak leaf lettuce or mignonette · 30g (1 oz) lamb's lettuce (corn salad) or purslane · few radicchio leaves · handful of rocket leaves · 2 heads chicory (witlof), sliced diagonally 4 tablespoons olive oil · 1 clove garlic, halved 2 slices bread, cut into cubes · 185g (6oz) wild mushrooms, such as ceps, chanterelles or field mushrooms · 125g (4oz) smoked bacon, rinds removed, cut into strips · 2 tablespoons raspberry wine vinegar · salt and pepper to taste

To Garnish:
few chives

1 Prepare all the salad leaves, tearing the frisée (endive) and larger leaves into smaller pieces. Place in a salad bowl and toss gently.

2 Heat the oil in a frying pan, add the garlic and bread cubes and fry until crisp and golden. Remove the bread cubes from the pan and keep warm.

3 Add the mushrooms and bacon to the pan and fry quickly for 5-6 minutes, stirring frequently, then remove with a slotted spoon and scatter over the salad. Discard the garlic.

4 Quickly pour the vinegar into the pan, stir to mix in the juices, then pour over the salad. Season well with salt and pepper and sprinkle with the croûtons. Garnish with chives to serve.

Serves 4

VARIATION: Replace the mushrooms with 185g (6oz) chicken livers. Fry with the bacon for 6-7 minutes, until tender but still slightly pink inside. Thinly slice after frying and scatter over the salad. Continue as above.

HOT CHICKEN & ROQUETTE SALAD

I love meals like this which are quickly cooked and can be eaten with just a fork, casually among friends. Wash it down with large glasses of Sancerre or Sauvignon wine!

125g (4oz) French beans, topped and tailed · 250g (8oz) roquette · 1 small onion, thinly sliced · 4-6 tablespoons olive or groundnut oil · 3 boneless chicken breasts, sliced · 60g (2oz/⅔ cup) walnut halves · 1-2 cloves garlic, crushed · 2 teaspoons shredded lemon rind · juice of 1 lemon · 1 teaspoon brown sugar · salt and pepper

To Garnish:
chopped parsley (optional)

1 Cook the French beans in boiling water for 2 minutes only. Refresh with cold water, drain and set aside. Arrange a bed of roquette and onion rings on 4 individual serving plates.

2 Heat 4 tablespoons oil in a wok or large frying pan. Add the chicken and stir-fry over a high heat for about 4 minutes until lightly browned. Add the walnuts and garlic and continue stir-frying for 2-3 minutes, adding more oil if necessary, until the chicken is cooked through.

3 Add the lemon rind and juice to the pan, together with the sugar and French beans. Continue cooking for 1 minute to heat through, then season with salt and pepper to taste. Spoon over the roquette and onion and serve immediately, sprinkled with chopped parsley if desired.

Serves 4

VARIATION: Replace the walnut halves with blanched almonds and use orange rind and juice instead of lemon.

MINTED LAMB & BULGHUR SALAD

Strips of tender pink lamb and Mediterranean vegetables tossed with bulghur wheat in a minted citrus dressing. For a perfect summer meal accompany with tzatziki – the Greek yogurt and cucumber dip – lots of bread and chilled white wine.

250g (8oz/1 1/3 cups) bulghur wheat · 375g (12oz) boneless lamb steaks · 4 tablespoons olive oil 1 small aubergine (eggplant), diced · 90g (3oz) button mushrooms, halved · 1/2 red pepper, finely diced · 1/2 green pepper, finely diced · 2 small courgettes (zucchini), thinly sliced

Dressing:
4 tablespoons olive oil · 2 tablespoons white wine vinegar · grated rind and juice of 1 lemon · 1 clove garlic, crushed · 2 tablespoons chopped mint · salt and pepper to taste

To Garnish:
mint sprigs

1 Put the bulghur wheat in a large bowl. Stir in 500ml (16 fl oz/2 cups) boiling water and leave to stand for 45 minutes, until all the liquid is absorbed.
2 Preheat the grill to high and grill the lamb steaks for 5-6 minutes, turning once, until well browned on the outside but still pink within. Transfer to a plate and allow to cool.
3 Heat the oil in a large frying pan, add the aubergine (eggplant) and mushrooms and sauté for 2-3 minutes, until just beginning to brown. Add to the bulghur wheat with the peppers and courgettes (zucchini). Slice the lamb thinly across the grain and add to the salad.
4 To make the dressing, stir all the ingredients together in a small bowl or shake in a screw-top jar until combined. Pour the dressing over the salad and toss gently to mix. Serve garnished with mint sprigs. **Serves 4**

VARIATION: For a seafood version, replace the lamb with large prawns and mussels, and mint with dill or parsley.

BEEF NIÇOISE

Rare cooked beef and new potatoes are particularly good flavoured with lots of wholegrain mustard. Here I have added French beans, tomatoes and olives for a superb and hearty Niçoise-style salad. Serve with French bread.

375g (12oz) beef fillet, cut into 2.5cm (1 inch) thick steaks · freshly ground black pepper · 500g (1lb) small new potatoes · 125g (4oz) French beans, topped and tailed · 16 green olives, preferably anchovy-stuffed · 4 tomatoes, skinned and quartered
½ red onion, sliced

Dressing:
5 tablespoons olive oil · 2 tablespoons red wine vinegar · ½ clove garlic, crushed · 3 teaspoons wholegrain mustard · pinch of sugar · salt to taste

To Garnish:
chopped parsley

1 Preheat the grill to high. Season the beef liberally with pepper and grill for about 5 minutes, turning once, until well browned on the outside but still rare inside. Transfer to a plate and allow to cool.
2 Meanwhile, cook the potatoes in boiling salted water for 10-12 minutes until just tender. Allow to cool, then halve. Blanch the beans in boiling water, then refresh in cold water and drain. Transfer the cooked potatoes and beans to a large salad bowl and add the olives, tomatoes and onion. Slice the beef thinly across the grain and add to the salad.
3 To make the dressing, stir all the ingredients together in a small bowl or shake in a screw-top jar until combined. Pour over the salad and toss gently to mix. Sprinkle with chopped parsley to garnish. **Serves 4**

GADO GADO

This crunchy Indonesian-style salad with its spicy peanut sauce will appeal to vegetarians and non-vegetarians alike. Include other vegetables if you prefer, such as French beans, baby corn cobs or cauliflower flowerets.

2 tablespoons groundnut or olive oil · 185g (6oz) firm tofu, diced · 1 clove garlic, halved · 185g (6oz) beansprouts · 185g (6oz) leek · 250g (8oz) carrot 250g (8oz) celery · 125g (4oz) mange tout (snow peas, topped and tailed · 185g (6oz) Chinese cabbage, shredded

Peanut Sauce:

30g (1oz) creamed coconut · 4 tablespoons milk ½ small onion, chopped · 1 clove garlic, crushed 4 tablespoons peanut butter · 1 teaspoon soft brown sugar · 2 teaspoons soy sauce · ½ teaspoon ground cumin · ½ teaspoon chilli powder

To Garnish:

1 egg, hard-boiled and finely chopped (optional)

1 First make the peanut sauce: chop the creamed coconut and place in a blender or food processor with the milk. Blend to a paste. Add the remaining sauce ingredients and purée until smooth.

2 Heat the oil in a frying pan, add the tofu and garlic and cook for 2-3 minutes, stirring gently, until the tofu is pale golden and beginning to crisp. Drain on absorbent kitchen paper and discard the garlic.

3 Arrange the beansprouts on a serving platter or in a shallow bowl.

4 Cut the leek, carrot and celery into julienne strips and blanch in boiling water for 1-2 minutes then refresh with cold water and drain thoroughly. Blanch the mange tout (snow peas) for 30 seconds; refresh and drain. Arrange the blanched vegetables, Chinese cabbage and tofu on top of the beansprouts.

5 To serve, spoon the peanut sauce over the middle of the salad. Sprinkle with chopped hard-boiled egg to garnish, if desired.

Serves 4

BROWN RICE SALAD

A substantial main course salad. For extra flavour, the rice is cooked as for a risotto – fried in a little butter, then simmered in stock. If available, use brown risotto rice for the best results.

30g (1 oz) butter · ½ small onion, chopped · 315g (10oz/1½ cups) brown rice · 125g (4oz) button mushrooms, quartered · 750ml (24 fl oz/3 cups) hot vegetable stock or water · 1 small green pepper, sliced · 1 small red pepper, sliced · 250g (8oz) frozen peas, thawed · 3 eggs, hard-boiled
2 tablespoons chopped parsley
salt and pepper to taste

Dressing:
6 tablespoons mayonnaise · 4 tablespoons single (light) cream · 1 teaspoon lemon juice
2 tablespoons snipped chives

To Garnish:
few chives · parsley sprigs

1 Heat the butter in a saucepan. Add the onion and fry gently for about 4 minutes until just beginning to brown. Stir in the rice and mushrooms and continue cooking, stirring constantly, for 2 minutes. Pour in the stock or water, bring to the boil, then cover and simmer gently for 20-25 minutes until all the liquid is absorbed.
2 Meanwhile to make the dressing, stir the ingredients together in a small bowl and set aside.
3 Stir the peppers and peas into the hot rice, transfer to a large bowl and leave to cool.
4 Chop 2 hard-boiled eggs and add to the salad with the parsley. Season with salt and pepper and toss gently to mix. Transfer to a serving dish and spoon over the dressing.
5 Slice the remaining hard-boiled egg and arrange on the salad. Garnish with chives and parsley. **Serves 4**

TOMATO & ROQUEFORT SALAD

This salad makes a truly delicious light vegetarian meal in its own right. Have plenty of warm crusty bread to hand.

1 head oakleaf or mignonette lettuce · 6 tomatoes, roughly chopped · ½ red onion, sliced · 16 black olives · 250g (8oz) Roquefort · 1 tablespoon each snipped chives, chervil and dill

Dressing:

3 tablespoons virgin olive oil · 3 tablespoons walnut oil · 3 tablespoons lemon juice · 1 tablespoon red wine vinegar · ½ clove garlic, crushed · pinch of sugar · salt and pepper to taste

1 Tear the lettuce into bite-sized pieces and put in a salad bowl with the tomatoes, onion and olives. Crumble in the Roquefort and add the herbs. Cover and chill until required.

2 To make the dressing, mix the ingredients together in a bowl or shake in a screw-top jar to combine. Pour over the salad and toss gently. **Serves 4**

BROCCOLI, BEAN & ALMOND SALAD

The Szechwan peppercorns used in the dressing for this colourful salad impart a wonderful aromatic flavour. If they are unavailable, you can use freshly ground pepper to taste instead.

185g (6oz/1 cup) red kidney beans, soaked overnight · 90g (3oz/½ cup) mung beans, soaked overnight · 375g (12oz) broccoli flowerets · 1 head radicchio · ½ head oakleaf, lollo rosso or mignonette lettuce · 60g (2oz/⅓ cup) blanched almonds, toasted · ½ red onion, sliced

Dressing:

5 tablespoons olive oil · 3 tablespoons raspberry vinegar · pinch of soft brown sugar · ½ teaspoon Szechwan peppercorns, crushed · salt to taste

1 Drain the beans, place in separate pans and cover with fresh water. Bring to the boil and boil rapidly for 10 minutes. Lower the heat, cover and simmer until tender: allow a further 40-50 minutes for kidney beans; 10-12 minutes for mung beans. Drain and rinse under cold running water to cool, then drain thoroughly and place in a large salad bowl.

2 Partly cook the broccoli in boiling water for 2 minutes, then drain and refresh with cold water. Drain well and add to the beans. Tear the salad leaves into bite-sized pieces and add to the salad with the almonds and onion.

3 To make the dressing, stir all the ingredients in a small bowl or shake in a screw-top jar to combine.

4 Just before serving pour the dressing over the salad and toss lightly to mix. **Serves 4**

PASTA SALAD WITH PESTO

Pesto – the traditional Italian basil sauce – is adapted here to make a delicious dressing for a vegetarian pasta salad. Flavoured bread, such as walnut, onion or olive, makes a perfect accompaniment if you can obtain one. Otherwise serve any warm crusty bread.

500g (1lb) dried pasta quills (penne) · 125g (4oz) French beans · 125g (4oz) cherry tomatoes, halved 60g (2oz) button mushrooms, sliced 30g (1oz/¼ cup) pine nuts, toasted · few black olives (optional)

Pesto Dressing:
8 tablespoons virgin olive oil · 30g (1oz) basil leaves 30g (1oz) Parmesan cheese, grated · 4 teaspoons white wine vinegar · 1 clove garlic, crushed pepper to taste

1 Cook the pasta in plenty of boiling salted water for 7-8 minutes, until *al dente*, tender but firm to the bite. Rinse under cold running water to cool, drain well and transfer to a large salad bowl.
2 Top and tail the beans, then blanch in boiling water for 1 minute. Refresh in cold water and drain. Add to the pasta with the cherry tomatoes, mushrooms, pine nuts and olives, if using.
3 To make the dressing, place all the ingredients in a blender or food processor and purée for a few seconds until the mixture is fairly smooth. Add to the salad and toss gently to mix. **Serves 4**

VARIATION: Substitute another pasta shape, such as shells or twists, or use wholewheat pasta if you prefer. For a more substantial vegetarian salad add 90g (3oz/¾ cup) cooked flageolet beans.

WHOLEWHEAT & FRUIT SALAD

Wholewheat – with its chewy texture and slightly nutty flavour – provides an excellent alternative to brown rice for vegetarian salads. I have chosen Wensleydale to complement the fruit but substitute your favourite cheese if you prefer.

185g (6oz/1 cup) wholewheat, soaked · 1 dessert apple · 1 ripe pear · 2 tablespoons lemon juice 90g (3oz) seedless red grapes · 2 sticks celery, cut into matchsticks · 60g (2oz/½ cup) dried apricots, chopped · 60 g (2oz/⅓ cup) pitted prunes, chopped 185g (6oz) Wensleydale cheese, cubed

Dressing:

5 tablespoons grapeseed oil · 2 tablespoons white wine vinegar · juice and grated rind of ½ orange 1 teaspoon chopped rosemary salt and pepper to taste

1 Drain the wholewheat and cook in boiling water for 20 minutes until just tender. Rinse under cold water, drain thoroughly and leave to cool. Transfer to a large salad bowl.

2 Halve and core the apple and pear. Slice the apple and dice the pear, sprinkling with lemon juice to prevent discolouring. Add to the wholewheat with the grapes, celery, apricots and prunes. Stir in the cheese cubes.

3 To make the dressing, stir all the ingredients together in a small bowl or shake in a screw-top jar until thoroughly combined. Pour the dressing over the salad and toss gently to mix. **Serves 4**

FLAGEOLET & FRENCH BEAN SALAD

A fresh-tasting, colourful salad flavoured with apricots, orange slices and walnuts.

250g (8oz) French beans · 1 × 470g (15oz) can flageolet beans, drained · about 60g (2oz) each frisée (endive) and oakleaf lettuce · 5 apricots, stoned and sliced · 1 orange, peeled and sliced 30g (1oz/¼ cup) walnut pieces

Dressing:

5 tablespoons olive oil · 3 tablespoons wine vinegar 1 teaspoon clear honey · 1 teaspoon grated orange rind · salt and pepper to taste

1 Trim the French beans and cook in boiling water for 3 minutes, then drain and refresh with cold water. Drain well and place in a serving bowl. Add the remaining ingredients.

2 To make the dressing, mix the ingredients together in a small bowl or shake in a screw-top jar to combine. Pour over the salad and toss lightly to mix. **Serves 4**

SUMMER SALAD WITH HERB TOASTS

Be generous with the garlic and fresh herbs used to make the hot little toasts that provide the perfect contrast to a crisp, fresh summer salad.

250g (8oz) asparagus spears · 90g (3oz) mange tout (snow peas) · 1 cos lettuce · ½ head frisée (curly endive) · 1 stick celery, cut into fine julienne 1 courgette (zucchini), cut into fine julienne 12 cherry tomatoes, halved

Dressing:
4 tablespoons olive or nut oil · 2 tablespoons white wine vinegar · pinch of salt · salt and pepper to taste

Herb Toasts:
1 thin French stick · 60g (2oz) butter, softened 1 tablespoon ground almonds · 2 cloves garlic, crushed · 3 tablespoons chopped mixed herbs, eg basil, tarragon, parsley, marjoram, chives

1 Break off and discard the woody ends of the asparagus. Peel the stalks and cut each spear in half. Cook in boiling water for 4-5 minutes only, then refresh with cold water, drain and allow to cool. Blanch the mange tout (snow peas) in boiling water for 1 minute, refresh and cool as above.
2 Tear the cos lettuce and frisée (endive) into bite-size pieces and place in a bowl with the asparagus, mange tout (snow peas), celery, courgette (zucchini) and tomatoes. Cover and chill until required.
3 To make the dressing, mix all the ingredients together in a small bowl or shake in a screw-top jar to combine.
4 For the herb toasts, cut the French stick into 2.5cm (1 inch) slices. In a bowl, blend together the butter, ground almonds, garlic and herbs.
5 Just before serving, preheat the grill and toast the bread until golden on both sides. Divide the garlic and herb butter between the hot toasts. Flash under the grill for a few seconds to heat through. Pour the dressing over the salad, toss lightly and serve immediately, with the herb toasts. **Serves 4**

WINTER GREEN SALAD

A crisp green salad tossed in a creamy dressing. Vary by including other winter vegetables, such as cauliflower, chicory (witlof) and green peppers, if you wish.

185g (6oz) hard white cabbage, shredded · 1 small fennel bulb, thinly sliced · 2 sticks celery, sliced 1 small leek, shredded · 1 green apple, cored and sliced

Dressing:
3 tablespoons mayonnaise · 2 tablespoons natural yogurt · ¼ teaspoon celery seed · salt and pepper to taste

To Garnish:
celery leaves

1 Divide all the salad ingredients between individual serving bowls.
2 To make the dressing, mix the ingredients together in a small bowl. Add to the salad and toss lightly. Garnish with celery leaves. **Serves 4-6**

VEGETABLE JULIENNE WITH HERBS

An attractive side salad of fine strips of vegetables tossed in a fresh herb dressing. You can vary the vegetables as you like. Try, for example, strips of fennel or cucumber.

3 celery sticks · 2 courgettes (zucchini) · 2 carrots
1 small leek, about 125g (4oz)

Dressing:
4 tablespoons olive oil · 2 tablespoons white wine vinegar · 6 teaspoons finely chopped mixed herbs, such as chives, parsley, chervil · ½ teaspoon grated lemon rind · pinch of sugar · salt and pepper to taste

To Garnish:
chervil or parsley sprigs

1 To make the dressing, mix the ingredients together in a small bowl or shake in a screw-top jar to combine.
2 Cut the vegetables into thin matchsticks, or 'julienne' and divide between individual salad bowls. Pour the dressing over and toss gently to mix. Garnish with chervil or parsley. **Serves 4-6**

SUMMER HERB SALAD WITH CROÛTONS

A leafy salad with an abundance of summer herbs and edible flowers, plus crisp croûtons for extra crunch. For a special touch cut out shaped croûtons; toss them into the salad at the last minute to ensure they stay crisp.

250g (8oz) mixed salad leaves, such as lamb's lettuce (corn salad), escarole, radicchio, frisée (endive), chicory (witlof), four seasons lettuce, watercress, nasturtium leaves · handful of herb sprigs, such as chervil, dill, fennel · 45g (1 ½ oz) edible flowers, such as nasturtium, borage, marigold

Dressing:

3 tablespoons olive oil · 2 tablespoons walnut oil 2 tablespoons wine vinegar · ¼ teaspoon Dijon mustard · salt and pepper to taste

Croûtons:

3 thick slices white bread, crusts removed 2-3 tablespoons olive oil · 30g (1 oz) butter

1 Place the salad leaves, herb sprigs and edible flowers in a large serving bowl.

2 To make the dressing, stir all the ingredients together in a small bowl or shake in a screw-top jar to combine. Set aside.

3 To make the croûtons, cut the bread into even-size cubes or cut into shapes using small pastry cutters. Heat the oil and butter in a frying pan until hot and sizzling. Add the bread and fry, stirring, for 3-4 minutes, until the croûtons are pale and golden and crisp. Drain on absorbent kitchen paper and season with salt to taste.

4 Just before serving, pour the dressing evenly over the salad and toss very lightly. Sprinkle the croûtons on top and serve immediately. **Serves 4-6**

GOURMET VEGETABLE SALAD

Tender young vegetables are lightly cooked and tossed in a cooled hollandaise sauce to give a salad accompaniment worthy of any gourmet. This is a simple, no-fail hollandaise.

250g (8oz) new potatoes · ½ cauliflower, cut into flowerets · 185g (6oz) baby carrots · 185g (6oz) courgettes (zucchini) · 185g (6oz) sugar snap peas 185g (6oz) asparagus spears

Hollandaise Sauce:

3 egg yolks · 1 teaspoon caster sugar · pinch of salt juice of 1 lemon · 2 tablespoons white wine vinegar 185g (6oz) butter · ½ clove garlic, crushed 1 tablespoon chopped chervil

To Garnish:

chervil sprigs

1 First make the hollandaise: blend the egg yolks, sugar and salt in a food processor or blender for 2 seconds to mix. In a small pan, heat the lemon juice and vinegar and, with the machine on high speed, drizzle onto the egg yolks.

2 In the same pan, heat the butter with the garlic and chervil until bubbling. Drizzle onto the egg mixture at high speed as before, to give a smooth thick sauce. Transfer to a bowl, cover the surface with plastic wrap and allow to cool.

3 Meanwhile, cook the potatoes in boiling salted water for 8-10 minutes until tender. Drain and cool; cut in half if large. Cook the cauliflower and carrots in boiling water for about 3 minutes until almost tender. Drain and cool.

4 Quarter the courgettes (zucchini) lengthwise and cut into 5cm (2 inch) lengths. Blanch, together with the sugar snap peas, in boiling water for 1 minute; rinse and drain.

5 Break off and discard the woody ends of the asparagus. using a potato peeler, peel the stalks and cut in half. Cook in boiling water for 4-5 minutes until just tender; rinse and drain.

6 Put all of the vegetables into a large salad bowl. Spoon over the hollandaise sauce and toss lightly. Garnish with chervil sprigs to serve. **Serves 6-8**

CHERRY TOMATO & BEAN SALAD

If you can find yellow cherry tomatoes, include some in this salad for extra colour.

185g (6oz) braod beans · 185g (6oz) French beans, halved · 125g (4oz) mozzarella cheese, cubed 500g (1lb) cherry tomatoes, halved · tiny basil leaves and/or thyme sprigs to taste

Dressing:

½ red pepper · 155ml (5 fl oz/⅔ cup) olive oil 1 clove garlic, crushed · 2 tablespoons dry white wine · 2 tablespoons lemon juice salt and pepper to taste

1 Cook the broad beans in plenty of boiling salted water for about 3 minutes; drain. Cook the French beans in boiling salted water for 7-10 minutes; drain.
2 Place the ingredients for the dressing in a food processor or blender and work until smooth. Pour into a salad bowl.
3 Toss in the broad beans, French beans, mozzarella, tomatoes and herbs. Cover and leave for at least 2 hours before serving. **Serves 6**

POTATO & WATERCRESS SALAD

This peppery salad is excellent served with barbecued meats or cold roast beef.

1.25kg (2½ lb) old potatoes · 1 bunch watercress, roughly chopped · ½ cucumber, peeled and sliced 1 small onion, finely chopped

Dressing:

315ml (10 fl oz/1¼ cups) mayonnaise
125ml (4 fl oz/½ cup) thick sour cream
2 tablespoons creamed horseradish · salt and pepper to taste

1 For the dressing, whisk together all the ingredients in a large bowl.

2 Cook the potatoes in boiling salted water until just tender. Drain well, thickly slice and toss immediately into the dressing; allow to cool.

3 Add the watercress, cucumber slices and chopped onion. Toss lightly to serve. **Serves 8**

AUBERGINE & MUSHROOM SALAD

This salad will keep in the refrigerator for a few days and makes a good accompaniment to cooked meats, or a delicious starter in its own right. Serve with crusty bread.

1 aubergine (eggplant), about 185g (6oz)
1 teaspoon salt · 1 teaspoon coriander seeds
½ teaspoon cumin seeds · ¼ teaspoon fenugreek
5 peppercorns · 6 tablespoons olive oil
2 cloves garlic, thinly sliced · 1 shallot, finely chopped · ½-1 red chilli, sliced · 185ml (6 fl oz/ ¾ cup) dry white wine · 375g (12oz) small whole button mushrooms · 2 tablespoons chopped coriander leaves

To Garnish:
coriander sprigs

1 Dice the aubergine (eggplant) and put in a colander. Rinse with cold water, then sprinkle with salt and leave to stand for 25-30 minutes to degorge. Rinse again to remove the salt.

2 Lightly crush the coriander seeds, cumin and fenugreek with the peppercorns.

3 Heat the oil in a large pan, add the garlic and shallot and cook, without browning, for 5-7 minutes. Add the crushed spices, chilli and aubergine (eggplant) and cook for 3 minutes, until the aubergine is just beginning to soften.

4 Stir in the wine and mushrooms. Bring to the boil, then remove from the heat and stir in the chopped coriander. Allow to cool, then cover and chill in the refrigerator for at least 2 hours before serving, garnished with coriander sprigs. **Serves 4-6**

FENNEL & PARMESAN SALAD

Wafer-thin slices of Parmesan and fennel complement each other perfectly in this salad. Make sure you use tender young spinach leaves.

90g (3oz) piece Parmesan cheese · 2 small fennel bulbs, thinly sliced · about 250g (8oz) young spinach leaves · 1 red onion, thinly sliced

Dressing:

4 tablespoons olive oil · 2 tablespoons lemon juice 2 tablespoons double (thick) cream · 1 tablespoon chopped fennel fronds · 1 teaspoon grated lemon rind · 1/4 teaspoon sugar · pepper to taste

1 Cut the Parmesan into wafer-thin slices and place in a bowl with the fennel. Toss lightly to mix.

2 Tear the spinach leaves roughly and arrange with the onion on individual serving plates. Pile the fennel and Parmesan mixture in the centre.

3 To make the dressing, stir all the ingredients together in a small bowl. Spoon the dressing over the salad just before serving, as an accompaniment to grilled or barbecued meat and fish. **Serves 4-6**

CUCUMBER & DILL SALAD

A delicate summery salad to accompany barbecued or grilled fish and chicken. If serving lamb, I use mint instead of dill.

1 cucumber · 2 teaspoons salt

Dressing:
3 tablespoons natural yogurt · 1 tablespoon double (thick) cream · 1 teaspoon chopped dill pepper to taste

To Garnish:
lightly crushed cumin seeds · dill sprigs

1 Using a potato peeler remove most of the peel from the cucumber in strips, then slice very thinly. Put in a colander and sprinkle with salt. Leave to stand for 20-30 minutes, then rinse thoroughly. Drain and place in a serving dish.

2 To make the dressing, stir all the ingredients together in a small bowl.

3 Spoon the dressing over the cucumber and sprinkle with cumin seeds. Garnish with dill. **Serves 4-6**

DATE & ORANGE SALAD

Peppery watercress and faintly bitter radicchio leaves are the perfect foil for fresh dates and sweet oranges in this colourful salad.

2 large oranges · 375g (12oz) fresh dates, halved and stoned · 1 head radicchio, roughly torn 60g (2oz) watercress sprigs

Dressing:

1 shallot, finely chopped · 4 tablespoons olive oil 2 tablespoons wine vinegar · 1 tablespoon chopped parsley · 2 teaspoons shredded orange rind pinch of sugar · salt and pepper to taste

1 Peel the oranges using a sharp knife to remove all the pith. Thinly slice and arrange in a shallow serving bowl with the dates, radicchio and watercress.

2 To make the dressing, stir all the ingredients in a small bowl or shake in a screw-top jar to combine. Spoon over the salad and serve immediately, as an accompaniment to chicken, duck or beef. **Serves 4-6**

BRUNCHES LUNCHES & SUPPERS

You will find plenty of imaginative ideas here for easy meals where speed is of the essence. Ideas range from triple-decker sandwiches and filled warm bagels to original omelettes, creamy scrambled eggs with smoked salmon, a classic Italian risotto, tempting pasta and pizzas.

CLASSIC CLUB SANDWICH

A three layer sandwich of smoked chicken, roast ham and salad. Eat it the American way – with a generous salad garnish.

250g (8oz) smoked chicken, chopped · 2 spring onions (green shallots), chopped · 3 tablespoons mayonnaise · salt and pepper · 75g (2½oz) butter 16 slices brown or white bread · wholegrain mustard to taste · 8 slices roast ham · 4 tomatoes, thinly sliced · about 60g (2oz) salad leaves

To Garnish:
lemon slices · mixed salad leaves · few radishes

1 In a small bowl, mix together the smoked chicken, spring onions (green shallots) and mayonnaise. Season with salt and pepper to taste.

2 Thinly butter each slice of bread on one side only. Place 4 slices, buttered side up, on a board. Spread with mustard to taste, then place a slice of roast ham on each. Divide half of the tomato slices and salad leaves between the bread slices, then add another layer of bread.

3 Divide the smoked chicken mixture between the sandwiches and top with another layer of bread. Spread with mustard and cover with the remaining ham, tomato and salad. Top with the final bread slices. Secure the sandwiches with cocktail sticks then cut into quarters. Serve garnished with lemon slices, mixed salad leaves and radishes. **Serves 4-6**

BACON, LETTUCE AND TOMATO SANDWICH 'BLT': Replace the smoked chicken filling with 8 rashers crispy grilled streaky bacon and 2 sliced tomatoes. In place of the roast ham and mustard, use 3 chopped hard-boiled eggs mixed with 3 tablespoons mayonnaise.

PAIN BAGNAT

This version of a traditional Provencal snack is made with tomato, onion, basil and brie. The bread must be 'bathed' in olive oil.

4 short French sticks or large crusty rolls
125ml (4 fl oz/1 cup) virgin olive oil · 1 clove garlic, crushed · salt and pepper to taste · 4 large tomatoes, thinly sliced · 1 onion, thinly sliced
315g (10oz) brie, thinly sliced · 3 tablespoons chopped basil · 6 black olives, stoned and sliced

1 Preheat the oven to 180C (350F/Gas 4). Cut the bread in half horizontally and sprinkle the cut sides with the olive oil, garlic, salt and pepper. Reassemble the loaves or rolls and place on a baking sheet. Bake in the oven for about 5 minutes until warmed.

2 Fill the French sticks or rolls with the tomato slices, onion rings, brie, chopped basil and sliced olives. Serve immediately. **Serves 4**

NEW YORK BAGELS

Whatever you fill bagels with, it's well worth warming them for a few minutes in the oven first. Each of the filling recipes here will generously fill 2 bagels. You can, of course, simply double up either filling to fill all 4 bagels.

4 bagels

Herring and Egg Filling:
2 eggs, hard-boiled and chopped · 3 tablespoons mayonnaise · 2 teaspoons chopped parsley · salt and pepper · 2 roll-mop herrings, sliced · few small parsley sprigs

Smoked Salmon Filling:
125g (4oz) cream cheese · 2 teaspoons snipped chives · 2 teaspoons lemon juice · freshly ground black pepper · 60g (2oz) smoked salmon slices

To Garnish:
lemon slices · chives · salad leaves

1 Preheat the oven to 180C (350F/Gas 4). Warm the bagels in the oven for 5 minutes, then cut in half horizontally.

2 To prepare the herring and egg filling, in a small bowl mix together the chopped eggs, mayonnaise and parsley. Season with salt and pepper to taste. Divide the egg mixture between 2 bagel bases. Slice the roll-mops and arrange on top of the egg, with parsley sprigs. Replace the bagel tops.

3 To prepare the smoked salmon filling, in a small bowl mix together the cream cheese, chives and lemon juice. Season with pepper to taste. Divide the cream cheese mixture between the remaining 2 bagel bases and arrange the smoked salmon on top. Replace the bagel tops.

4 Serve the bagels garnished with lemon slices, chives and salad leaves.

Serves 4

SMOKED SALMON & ASPARAGUS EGGS

Serve this extravagant brunch or supper dish with slices of toasted brioche, and with orange juice, white wine or champagne to accompany. You could round off the meal with fresh strawberries and cream.

375g (12oz) thin asparagus spears · 185g (6oz) sliced smoked salmon · 6 eggs · salt and pepper to taste · 15-30g (½-1oz) butter · 3 tablespoons single (light) cream

To Serve:
chervil sprigs to garnish · 4 slices brioche, toasted

1 Break off and discard the woody stalk ends of the asparagus and, using a potato peeler, thinly peel the stems. Cut each asparagus spear in half. Cook in boiling water for about 5 minutes until just tender. Drain well and keep hot.

2 Arrange half of the smoked salmon and two thirds of the asparagus on individual serving plates. Roughly chop the remaining salmon and asparagus.

3 Beat the eggs in a bowl. Season with salt and pepper. Melt the butter in a non-stick saucepan over a low heat. Add the eggs and cook, stirring lightly with a wooden spoon, for about 3 minutes, until they begin to thicken and set; take care not to overcook – the eggs should be creamy and soft. Stir in the chopped asparagus, chopped smoked salmon and the cream.

4 Divide the scrambled egg and smoked salmon mixture between the serving plates and serve immediately, garnished with chervil sprigs and accompanied by slices of toasted brioche.

Serves 4

ORIENTAL OMELETTE

This omelette is topped with a tasty stir-fry – inspired by the ingredients typically found in egg-fried rice.

4 eggs · 15-30g (½-1oz) butter

Filling:

2 tablespoons oil · 1 clove garlic, crushed · 1 carrot, cut into thin strips · 2 spring onions (green shallots), sliced · 90g (3oz) mange tout (snow peas), topped and tailed · 6 water chestnuts, chopped 125g (4oz) peeled prawns · handful of coriander leaves · 2 teaspoons light soy sauce

1 First prepare the filling. Heat the oil in a non-stick frying pan. Add the garlic, carrot and spring onion (shallot) and stir-fry for 2 minutes. Add the mange tout (snow peas) and cook for 1 minute. Stir in the remaining ingredients; heat through. Transfer to a bowl; keep hot.
2 To make the omelette, beat the eggs with 4 tablespoons water. Melt half the butter in the non-stick frying pan and pour in half of the egg mixture. As the edges of the omelette set, push them towards the centre with a spatula, allowing the runny mixture to fill the pan. Continue cooking in this way until the omelette is just set. Transfer to a warmed plate and repeat with the remaining egg mixture.
3 Divide the stir-fry between the omelettes and serve immediately. **Serves 2**

VARIATION: To make a mushroom filling, melt 15g (½oz) butter in a small pan, add 1 halved garlic clove and 1 chopped shallot and cook gently for 2 minutes; discard garlic. Stir in 250g (8oz) sliced mushrooms and cook for 4-5 minutes. Remove from the heat and stir in a little cream. Fold the omelettes to enclose filling.

MUFFINS FLORENTINE

Toasted muffins – topped with spinach in a creamy mustard sauce and softly poached eggs – make a perfect brunch or fast supper.

4 muffins · 4 eggs · 2 tablespoons vinegar (optional)
30g (1oz) butter · 375g (12oz) spinach leaves, shredded · 90ml (3 fl oz/⅓ cup) double (thick) cream · 2-3 teaspoons wholegrain mustard
2 teaspoons chopped parsley · salt and pepper

To Garnish:
paprika for sprinkling · parsley sprigs
stuffed green olives

1 Split the muffins and toast on both sides. Keep warm.
2 Cook the eggs in a poaching pan over hot water, for about 4 minutes. Alternatively pour water into a large saucepan to a depth of 5cm (2 inches). Add the vinegar and bring to the boil, then lower the heat to a gentle simmer. Crack an egg on to a saucer and gently slide into the pan. Repeat with another egg. Cook 2 eggs at a time for 3-4 minutes until softly set. Set aside and keep warm while cooking the other 2 eggs.
3 Melt the butter in a saucepan, add the spinach and cook, stirring, for 1-2 minutes until just wilted. Drain off any excess liquid, then stir in the cream, mustard and parsley. Heat through for a few seconds and season with salt and pepper to taste.
4 To serve, arrange 2 muffin halves on each individual serving plate, and spoon over the creamed spinach. Top each serving with a poached egg and sprinkle with paprika. Serve immediately, garnished with parsley sprigs and stuffed olives. **Serves 4**

BLUE BRIE & WATERCRESS TART

Make this tart ahead, if you like, and serve it warm or cold with a leafy salad. You can use a plain creamy Brie if you prefer.

Pastry:
250g (8oz/2 cups) plain flour · pinch of salt 125g (4oz) butter or margarine · 3 tablespoons cold water (approximately)

Filling:
30g (1oz) butter · 2 bunches watercress, stalks removed · 315g (10oz) blue brie, rind removed, diced · 3 eggs · 155ml (5 fl oz/⅔ cup) single (light) cream · salt and pepper to taste

1 Preheat oven to 200C (400F/Gas 6). To make the pastry, sift the flour and salt into a large bowl. Rub in the butter or margarine until the mixture resembles breadcrumbs. Add the water and mix to a firm dough.
2 Roll out the pastry on a lightly floured surface and use to line an oiled 20cm (8 inch) flan tin. Prick the base and chill for 15 minutes, then bake blind in the preheated oven for 10-12 minutes. Lower the oven temperature to 180C (350F/Gas 4).
3 Meanwhile prepare the filling. Melt the butter in a large frying pan, add the watercress and cook, stirring, for 1-2 minutes until just wilted. Drain in a sieve, pressing out excess liquid, then arrange in the pastry case. Tuck the brie cubes into the watercress.
4 Beat together the eggs and cream, season with salt and pepper and pour into the flan. Bake in the oven for 30-35 minutes or until set. Serve warm, for preference, or cold, with salad. **Serves 4-6**

GRILLED RADICCHIO & CHÈVRE

Choose chèvre (goat's cheese) which has a 'rind' on the outside for this recipe; it will help the cheese keep its shape when melting.
Buy artichoke hearts, preserved in oil, from Italian delicatessens. Crusty granary bread is the perfect accompaniment for this light meal.

3 heads radicchio, quartered · 4 tablespoons olive oil · salt and pepper · 185g (6oz) chèvre (goat's cheese) log, sliced · 6 preserved artichoke hearts
2 tablespoons capers · 2 tablespoons walnut oil
1 tablespoon chopped basil or oregano

To Garnish:
basil sprigs

1 Preheat the grill. Place the radicchio on a baking sheet, sprinkle with the olive oil and season with salt and pepper to taste. Cook under the preheated grill for 8-10 minutes, turning frequently, until well browned.
2 After 5 minutes of the radicchio cooking time, add the chèvre (goat's cheese) to the grill and cook for 3-5 minutes, until well browned and sizzling.
3 Meanwhile, drain the artichoke hearts.
4 Arrange the radicchio, chèvre (goat's cheese) and artichoke hearts on individual serving plates. Sprinkle with the capers, walnut oil and chopped basil or oregano. Serve immediately, garnished with basil, and accompanied by crusty granary bread. **Serves 4**

VARIATION: Try substituting plump heads of chicory (witlof) for the radicchio in this recipe. Like radicchio, chicory (witlof) has a slightly bitter flavour which is mellowed by grilling to delicious effect.

LEEK & STILTON SOUFFLÉ

A successful well-risen soufflé is not as difficult to prepare as many people imagine. Be confident – don't keep nervously opening the oven door – and have a simple green or tomato salad ready and waiting to accompany.

60g (2oz) butter · 250g (8oz) leeks, finely chopped 6 teaspoons plain flour · 140ml (4½ fl oz/½ cup + 1 tablespoon) milk · 185g (6oz) blue Stilton cheese, grated · ½ teaspoon powdered mustard salt and pepper to taste · 4 eggs, separated

1 Preheat the oven to 190C (375F/Gas 5). Melt the butter in a saucepan. Add the leeks and sauté over a gentle heat for 2-3 minutes to soften. Stir in the flour and cook for 1 minute, stirring.

2 Remove the pan from the heat and gradually stir in the milk. Return to the heat and bring to the boil, stirring constantly; cook, stirring, until thickened. Stir in the cheese and mustard and season with salt and pepper. Allow to cool slightly, then stir in the egg yolks.

3 Whisk the egg whites until stiff peaks form. Stir a little of the whisked egg whites into the sauce to lighten the mixture, then carefully fold in the remainder.

4 Spoon the mixture into an oiled 1.25 litre (40 fl oz/ 5 cup) soufflé dish and bake in the centre of the preheated oven for 40-50 minutes, until well risen, golden brown and just firm. Serve immediately. **Serves 4**

INDIVIDUAL SOUFFLÉS: Divide the soufflé mixture between 4 oiled 315ml (10 fl oz/1¼ cup) individual soufflé dishes. Bake at 190C (375F/Gas 5) for 25 minutes.

ROSTI & SALAD

A light, fresh salad enhanced by a walnut oil dressing is served on top of a hot, crisp potato cake.

Rosti:

1kg (2lb) potatoes, peeled · 3 tablespoons olive oil
1 small onion, finely chopped · salt and pepper to taste · 30g (1oz) butter

Salad:

about 185g (6oz) mixed salad leaves, eg frisée (curly endive), lamb's lettuce (corn salad), chicory (witlof) · 125g (4oz) carrot, cut into julienne strips
1 courgette (zucchini), cut into julienne strips
2 teaspoons chopped parsley or chervil

Dressing:

2 tablespoons olive oil · 2 tablespoons walnut oil
2 tablespoons wine vinegar · ½ teaspoon French mustard · ½ teaspoon sugar · salt and pepper to taste

To Garnish:

parsley or chervil sprigs

1 Partially cook the potatoes in boiling salted water for about 8 minutes. Drain and allow to cool.

2 Meanwhile heat 1 tablespoon oil in a medium frying pan. Add the onion and cook gently for 3 minutes until softened but not browned. Coarsely grate the potatoes into a large bowl. Add the onion and seasoning; mix well.

3 To prepare the salad, combine the salad leaves, carrot, courgette (zucchini) and herbs in a large bowl; cover and chill until required. Mix the dressing ingredients together in a small bowl or shake in a screw-top jar to combine.

4 To prepare the rosti, divide the potato mixture into 4 portions. Heat ½ tablespoon olive oil and a little butter in the frying pan until hot and sizzling. Add a potato portion to the pan and flatten firmly to form a 'cake'. Cook over a medium heat for 8-10 minutes, turning once, until golden. Transfer to a plate and keep hot while preparing the others. Repeat to make 4 rosti.

5 To serve, place the rosti on warmed individual serving plates. Add the dressing to the salad, toss well and pile on top of the rosti. Serve immediately, garnished with herb sprigs.

Serves 4

GREEN RISOTTO

A pretty risotto, well flavoured with fresh herbs, asparagus, broccoli and Parmesan. Arborio rice is the only rice that will give the correct creaminess to the risotto. Don't rush the pouring in of stock or you will have crunchy watery rice!

60g (2oz) butter · 1 onion, finely chopped
625ml (1 pint/2½ cups) chicken or vegetable stock
375g (12oz) mixed broccoli florets and asparagus
280ml (9 fl oz/1 cup + 2tbsp) white wine
185g (6oz/1 cup) arborio or risotto rice
4-6 tablespoons chopped mixed herbs
4 tablespoons finely pared Parmesan cheese

To Garnish:
parsley sprigs

1 Melt the butter in a saucepan, add the onion and cook gently for 5 minutes until soft, but not coloured.
2 Meanwhile, bring the stock to the boil in another pan. Add the green vegetables and simmer for 3 minutes; remove the vegetables with a slotted spoon and reserve. Pour the wine into the stock and keep simmering.
3 Add the rice to the onion and stir to coat. Add a ladleful of stock and stir gently over a low heat until absorbed. Repeat, ladleful at a time, until all the stock is absorbed and the rice is tender and creamy. Stir in the vegetables and herbs and heat through.
4 Transfer to warmed individual serving dishes and add the Parmesan. Serve immediately, garnished with parsley.

Serves 3-4

PASTA WITH PARMA HAM & CHEESE

I love the flavour and papery, crisp texture of cooked Parma ham. Here I have combined it with some of my other favourites – pasta and sizzling grilled goat's cheese. Offset the richness of this dish with a simple salad.

500g (1 lb) paglio e fieno (fine green and white noodles) or spinach and egg tagliatelle · salt and pepper to taste · 185g (6oz) Parma ham, cut into ribbons or long wide strips · 250g (8oz) goat's cheese, such as montrachet, or crottin de chavignol, sliced · 3 tablespoons virgin olive oil
1-2 cloves garlic, crushed · 3 tablespoons chopped basil or marjoram

To Garnish:
basil or marjoram sprigs

1 Cook the pasta in plenty of boiling salted water for 2-4 minutes or until 'al dente'; drain well.
2 Meanwhile, line the grill pan with aluminium foil and preheat the grill. Arrange the Parma ham and goat's cheese slices on the foil and cook under the preheated grill for 2-3 minutes, until both are browned and sizzling, turning once.
3 Heat the olive oil in a large pan, add the garlic and fry gently for 1 minute. Remove from the heat and add the pasta to the pan, with the chopped basil or marjoram. Season with salt and pepper and toss gently to mix.
4 Divide the pasta between warmed individual serving plates and top each portion with grilled Parma ham and cheese. Serve immediately, garnished with sprigs of basil or marjoram. **Serves 4**

VARIATION: Omit the goat's cheese. Toss the pasta with 250g (8oz) steamed fine asparagus spears. Top with the Parma ham and serve with plenty of freshly grated Parmesan.

ONION & THREE CHEESE PIZZA

Pizza made with real, fresh dough takes less time to prepare than you might think. This dough only needs to rise once and makes 2 pizzas which will generously serve 4 to 6 people accompanied by a simple salad.

Pizza Dough:
15g (½ oz) dried yeast · 125ml (4 fl oz/½ cup) warm water · 500g (1lb/4 cups) plain flour good pinch of salt · 2 tablespoons olive oil

Topping:
45g (1½oz) butter · 2 large onions, sliced 3 tomatoes, skinned and chopped · 2 tablespoons chopped basil or marjoram · 125g (4oz) Roquefort or other blue cheese, crumbled 125g (4oz) mozzarella, sliced · 125g (4oz) red Leicester cheese, grated

1 To prepare the dough, dissolve the yeast in the water in a cup. Sift the flour and salt into a bowl, then stir in the oil and yeast liquid, adding a little extra water if necessary to give a smooth dough. Knead well, then divide in half and roll into two 20cm (8 inch) circles. Place on oiled baking sheets, cover loosely with plastic wrap and leave to rise in a warm place for 20 minutes.
2 Meanwhile, preheat the oven to 200C (400F/Gas 6). Melt the butter in a large frying pan, add the onions and fry gently for 10 minutes.
3 Divide the tomatoes and the onion mixture between the 2 pizza bases. Sprinkle each with basil or marjoram. Arrange the cheeses on top and bake in the preheated oven for 25-30 minutes. **Serves 4-6**

VARIATION: Omit the Roquefort and red Leicester cheeses. Increase the mozzarella to 185g (6oz) and arrange evenly over the pizzas. Top with anchovy fillets and black olives, or slices of salami and capers. Drizzle with a little olive oil and cook as above.

GARLIC & GOAT'S CHEESE PIZZETTE

This is one of my favourite recipes, derived from one of my favourite restaurant menus in London. You *have* to use whole garlic cloves, or slices at least, for the full effect – just hold your breath the next day!

1 large red pepper · 1 large yellow pepper
250g (8oz) packet pizza base mix · 1 large beef tomato · 8-12 cloves garlic, peeled · 125g (4oz) fresh Welsh or Somerset goat's cheese
salt and pepper to taste · olive oil for drizzling
2 tablespoons oregano or basil leaves

1 Preheat the oven to 240C (475F/Gas 9); preheat the grill, too. Grill the peppers, turning occasionally, until blackened all over. Slip off the skins under cold water and remove the stalks and seeds. Cut into strips.
2 Make up the pizza dough following the manufacturer's instructions. Divide into 4 pieces and roll out each one thinly to a 13cm (5 inch) round on a lightly floured surface. Place on a baking sheet.
3 Dip the tomato into boiling water for a count of ten. Lift out and plunge into cold water to stop further cooking. Peel the tomato, halve and remove the core and seeds. Roughly chop the flesh.
4 Scatter the chopped tomato over the pizzette. Top with pepper strips, garlic cloves and crumbled goat's cheese. Add seasoning and drizzle with olive oil. Bake in the oven for 10-15 minutes, until bubbling. Slide the pizzette on to individual serving plates and scatter with herbs. Serve immediately. **Serves 4**

HAM & ASPARAGUS GRATIN

Choose plump green or white asparagus spears for this dish. Serve with new potatoes and a crisp salad garnish.

12 large asparagus spears · 6 slices roast ham
30g (1oz/½ cup) fresh white breadcrumbs
30g (1oz/¼ cup) slivered almonds

Sauce:
45g (1½oz) butter · 45g (1½oz/⅓ cup) plain flour
470ml (15 fl oz/1¾ cups) milk · 90g (3oz) gruyére or mature Cheddar cheese · 2 teaspoons Dijon mustard · salt and pepper

1 To make the sauce, melt the butter in a small saucepan. Add the flour and cook for 1 minute, stirring. Remove from the heat and gradually stir in the milk. Return to the heat and cook, stirring constantly, to give a smooth sauce. Stir in the cheese and mustard, and season with salt and pepper to taste. Remove from the heat and set aside.

2 Break off and discard the woody ends of the asparagus spears. Using a potato peeler, thinly peel the stems. Cook the asparagus in boiling water for 4 minutes, then drain.

3 Preheat the oven to 190C (375F/Gas 5). Cut the ham slices in half and wrap each piece around an asparagus stem. Arrange the ham and asparagus rolls in a lightly greased baking dish. Spoon over the sauce and sprinkle with the breadcrumbs and almonds. Bake in the preheated oven for about 20 minutes until the sauce is hot and bubbling and the topping is browned and crisp. Serve immediately. **Serves 4**

MEDITERRANEAN KEBABS

You can serve these kebabs with pasta or rice, but they are substantial enough with just a salad.

500g (1 lb) boneless chicken breasts, skinned · 8 cooked Mediterranean (king) prawns · 8 bay leaves · 2 courgettes (zucchini) · 1 yellow pepper

Marinade:

4 tablespoons olive oil · juice of 1 lemon · 1 teaspoon finely grated lemon rind · ½ onion, finely chopped · 1 clove garlic, crushed · 2 teaspoons chopped dill or basil · salt and pepper to taste

1 Mix all the marinade ingredients together in a small bowl.

2 Cut the chicken into bite-size pieces and put in to a bowl with the prawns and bay leaves. Pour over the marinade and leave in the refrigerator for at least 1 hour.

3 Preheat the grill. Lift the chicken, prawns and bay leaves out of the marinade with a slotted spoon, reserving the marinade. Cut the courgettes (zucchini) and yellow pepper into 2.5cm (1 inch) pieces. Thread the courgettes (zucchini), pepper, prawns, bay leaves and chicken alternately on to 4 long skewers.

4 Brush the kebabs liberally with the marinade and cook under the hot grill for 7-10 minutes, until the chicken is cooked through, turning once and basting frequently with the marinade. Serve immediately with salad, pasta or rice. **Serves 4**

FISH & SHELLFISH

A fabulous selection of seafood recipes, cleverly flavoured with tasty marinades and sublime sauces. Everyday ideas include braised fish steaks, grilled fish and tasty kebabs. For special occasions, choose an elegant celebration salmon, lavish seafood platter or – in the height of summer – an exquisite barbecued whole fish.

MOUCLADE

This mussel stew from Brittany makes a delicious change from *moules marinière*. It is quite rich, so serve with plenty of crusty bread, followed by a light salad perhaps.

2.25 litres (4 pints/10 cups) mussels in shells
155ml (5 fl oz/⅔ cup) dry white wine · 2 shallots, finely chopped · 30g (1 oz) butter · 2 cloves garlic, crushed · 2 teaspoons potato flour or cornflour
315ml (10 fl oz/1¼ cups) double (thick) cream
pinch of saffron threads · salt and pepper to taste
juice of ½ lemon (approximately) · 1 egg yolk
1 tablespoon chopped parsley

To Garnish:
parsley sprigs

1 Scrub the mussels, removing the beards, and rinse well. Leave to soak in a bowl of cold water for 30 minutes, then tap each mussel sharply; discard any that do not close straight away.

2 Drain the mussels and place in a large saucepan. Add the wine and shallots, cover and cook over a high heat, shaking the pan frequently, for 5-10 minutes until the mussels open; discard any that remain closed at this stage.

3 Drain the mussels, reserving the liquid. Remove all empty half shells and keep the mussels warm. Boil the reserved liquid rapidly until reduced by half.

4 Melt the butter in a saucepan, add the garlic and cook until golden. Add the flour, then gradually stir in the reserved liquid. Add the cream, saffron and seasoning and simmer until slightly thickened. Add lemon juice to taste and stir in the egg yolk.

5 Divide the mussels between individual serving bowls and pour the sauce over them. Sprinkle with parsley and garnish with extra sprigs. Serve immediately, with lots of crusty bread. **Serves 3-4**

SPAGHETTI ALLE VONGOLE

A quick, easy pasta lunch or supper, with a Mediterranean flavour. Use fresh plum tomatoes, if possible. If fresh baby clams are not available hunt out jars or cans of clams in shells at your local Italian delicatessen – they make all the difference to this dish.

1kg (2lb) fresh baby clams, scrubbed, or 315g (10oz) can baby clams in shells plus 315g (10oz) can shelled clams · 5 tablespoons olive oil · 2 cloves garlic, crushed · 500g (1lb) tomatoes, skinned and chopped · 2 teaspoons tomato purée (paste) 1 tablespoon chopped parsley · salt and pepper 375g (12oz) spaghetti

To Garnish:
flat-leaved parsley sprigs

1 If using fresh clams, put them in a large pan with 7 tablespoons water. Cook, covered, over a high heat for 2-3 minutes until the shells open; discard any that remain closed. Strain, reserving the cooking liquid. Remove and discard the shells of half of the clams. If using canned clams, drain both types, reserving 6 tablespoons liquid.

2 Heat the oil in a large saucepan. Add the garlic and fry gently for 3-4 minutes. Stir in the tomatoes, tomato purée (paste) and clam liquid and simmer for 10 minutes. Add the clams and parsley and heat through for 1 minute. Season with salt and pepper to taste.

3 Meanwhile, cook the spaghetti in plenty of boiling salted water for 7-9 minutes or until 'al dente'. Drain thoroughly.

4 To serve, pile the spaghetti into warmed individual serving bowls, add the clam sauce and toss gently to mix. Garnish with parsley. **Serves 4**

SHELLFISH SALAD

Queen scallops – the tiny ones which are usually cheaper than ordinary scallops – can be used whole for this recipe instead of the familiar larger ones; you will need approximately 250g (8oz) in weight. The shellfish cooking liquor makes an excellent base for a fish soup, so I usually freeze this for later use.

8 shelled scallops, cleaned · 500g (1 lb) mussels in shells · 1 avocado · 375g (12oz) peeled prawns
2 tomatoes, skinned and cut into strips
250g (8oz/1½ cups) cooked rice · 2 tablespoons chopped chives · 2 tablespoons chopped chervil

Lemon Dressing:
4 tablespoons olive oil · 2 tablespoons lemon juice
1 clove garlic, crushed · salt and pepper to taste

To Garnish:
dill sprigs

1 Put the scallops into a pan, add sufficient water to three-quarters cover them and bring almost to the boil. Simmer gently for 2 minutes, then leave to cool. Drain, then cut each scallop into 3 pieces.

2 To clean the mussels, scrub them thoroughly under cold running water, removing the beards and discarding any mussels which stay open when tapped.

3 Bring 155ml (5 fl oz/⅔ cup) water to the boil in a large pan. Add the mussels, cover and cook briskly, shaking the pan occasionally, for 2-3 minutes until the shells open; discard any that remain closed. Cool slightly, then remove the mussels from their shells.

4 To make the dressing, put all the ingredients in a screw-topped jar and shake vigorously to combine.

5 Halve, stone and peel the avocado, then cut into chunks.

6 Combine the shelled mussels, scallops, prawns, tomatoes, avocado, rice and herbs in a bowl. Pour over the salad dressing and toss gently. Leave for about 1 hour before serving to allow the flavours to mingle. To serve, garnish with dill. **Serves 4**

FRUITS DE LA MER

A lavish special occasion seafood selection served with mayonnaise flavoured with lemon, tarragon and dill. Vary the seafoods as you like to include other fish goujons, lobster, oysters, etc.

90g (3oz/½ cup) dry white breadcrumbs
1 teaspoon garlic salt · 1 teaspoon finely grated lemon rind · 1 egg · 375g (12oz) mixed fish fillets, such as lemon sole and salmon · oil for deep frying
155ml (5 fl oz/⅔ cup) each dry white wine and water · 375g (12oz) squid, cleaned and sliced
500g (1lb) mussels in shells, scrubbed · 6 cooked crab claws · 12 cooked Mediterranean (king) prawns

Dressing:
155ml (5 fl oz/⅔ cup) mayonnaise · 2 teaspoons finely grated lemon rind · 1 tablespoon chopped dill
1 tablespoon chopped tarragon

To Garnish:
lemon slices · dill and tarragon sprigs

1 To prepare the fish goujons, mix together the breadcrumbs, garlic salt and grated lemon rind in a shallow bowl. Beat the egg lightly in a separate bowl. Cut the fish into strips and dip each first in egg, then in the breadcrumb mixture to coat evenly. Deep fry in batches in hot oil for 1-2 minutes until crisp, golden and cooked right through. Drain on absorbent kitchen paper and allow to cool.

2 Put the white wine and water in a saucepan and bring to the boil. Add the squid and cook for 2-3 minutes until tender then remove with a slotted spoon and leave to cool. Add the mussels to the pan and cook for 2-3 minutes until the shells have opened. Drain, discarding any unopened ones.

3 Arrange the prepared fish goujons, squid and mussels on a large serving platter together with the crab claws and prawns. Garnish with lemon slices, dill and tarragon.

4 To make the dressing, stir together the mayonnaise, lemon rind and chopped herbs in a small bowl. Serve with the seafood platter. **Serves 6**

KING PRAWNS WITH ASPARAGUS

A tangy lemony tarragon dressing enhances an already superb combination of asparagus, bacon and king prawns. Serve with crusty bread.

500g (1lb) asparagus · 6 rashers streaky bacon, rinds removed · 12-16 cooked Mediterranean (king) prawns, peeled · ½ head red oakleaf or mignonette lettuce, torn into bite-sized pieces · about 60g (2oz) lamb's lettuce (corn salad) or roquette

Dressing:

4 tablespoons olive oil · 3 tablespoons tarragon vinegar · 1 tablespoon lemon juice · 2 tablespoons chopped tarragon · salt and pepper to taste

1 To make the dressing, stir all the ingredients together in a small bowl or shake in a screw-top jar until combined. Set aside.

2 Halve the asparagus spears and cook in boiling salted water for 4-6 minutes, until just tender. Rinse under cold running water, drain and transfer to a bowl.

3 Preheat the grill to medium high. Cut the bacon rashers in half and wrap a half rasher around each prawn. Place on a foil-lined grill rack and grill for 3-4 minutes, turning once, until the bacon is crisp and the prawns are hot.

4 While the prawns are cooking, arrange the salad leaves on individual serving plates.

5 Add the cooked prawns and any cooking juices to the asparagus. Pour over the prepared dressing and toss lightly to mix. Arrange on top of the salad leaves and serve immediately.

Serves 4

VARIATION: When asparagus is not in season, or for a less expensive alternative, substitute 250g (8oz) mange tout (snow peas). Blanch for 1 minute only, then refresh as above.

MARINATED PRAWNS & CRAB CLAWS

These skewers are ideal for a special barbecue party and they can be prepared well ahead, to the end of stage 3. An aromatic saffron flavoured mayonnaise (see right) is the perfect complement.

1kg (2lb) medium-sized raw prawns, tails shelled
12 cooked crab claws
90g (3 oz/¾ cup) dry breadcrumbs

Marinade:
60ml (2 fl oz/¼ cup) olive oil · 60ml (2 fl oz/¼ cup) grapeseed oil · grated rind of 1 lemon 1 clove garlic, crushed · 2.5cm (1 inch) piece fresh root (green) ginger, chopped · 2 tablespoons white wine vinegar · large pinch of chilli powder 1 teaspoon paprika · salt and pepper to taste

To Garnish:
lemon slices

1 Whisk together the marinade ingredients in a bowl.
2 Peel the prawns, leaving the tails on, and place in a large non-metallic dish. Pour over all but 4 tablespoons of the marinade. Cover the dish.
3 Crack the crab claw shells by tapping them lightly with a rolling pin. Peel away the shell to expose the flesh but leave 2.5cm (1 inch) of shell at the tip. Place in a separate dish and spoon the reserved marinade over the crab flesh. Cover and leave both the prawns and crab claws in the refrigerator overnight.
4 Drain the prawns, reserving the marinade. Thread on to small wooden skewers and toss in the breadcrumbs. Barbecue or grill for about 2 minutes on each side, basting occasionally with the marinade.
5 Arrange the crab claws and prawns on a serving platter and garnish with lemon slices. Serve accompanied by the saffron mayonnaise. **Serves 6**

SAFFRON MAYONNAISE: Mix 315ml (10 fl oz/1¼ cups) mayonnaise with 250g (8oz) Greek yogurt. Sauté ½ onion, chopped, 1 crushed garlic clove and ½ teaspoon saffron powder in a little butter until soft. Add to the mayonnaise and purée in a blender or food processor.

ROLL-MOPS WITH APPLE

This salad makes a tasty lunch served with new potatoes or pumpernickel bread.

8 roll-mop herrings, halved · ½ red oakleaf lettuce
2 spring onions (green shallots), sliced
1 red apple, cored, halved and thinly sliced
2 sticks celery, sliced

Dressing:
4 tablespoons soured cream or natural yogurt
2 tablespoons mayonnaise · 1 teaspoon lemon juice
pinch of sugar · salt and pepper to taste

To Garnish:
pinch of paprika

1 Arrange the roll-mops, oakleaf lettuce, spring onions (shallots), apple and celery on individual serving plates.
2 To make the dressing, stir all the ingredients together in a small bowl.
3 Spoon the dressing over the salad and sprinkle with paprika to serve. **Serves 4**

SCALLOP & AVOCADO SALAD

This is an ideal dish for a light summer lunch party. Keep it simple and serve with a platter of smoked fish e.g. salmon, trout etc, a large mixed salad and plenty of interesting breads to accompany. Use fresh or frozen and thawed scallops.

1 kg (2 lb) scallops, halved horizontally · 1 large red pepper, cored, seeded and cut into thin strips
1 large green pepper, cored, seeded and cut into thin strips · 250g (8oz) red onion, thinly sliced
2 avocados · 500g (1 lb) tomatoes, peeled, seeded and cut into strips

Marinade:
1 clove garlic, crushed · 2 tablespoons soft brown sugar · 2 tablespoons chopped coriander
2 tablespoons chopped parsley · ½ teaspoon salt
½ teaspoon coarse-ground black pepper
75ml (2½ fl oz/⅓ cup) fresh lime juice
155ml (5 fl oz/⅔ cup) lemon juice

To Garnish:
parsley or coriander sprigs · shredded lemon zest
thin lime slices

1 For the marinade, whisk all of the ingredients together in a small bowl.
2 Place the scallops, peppers and onion in a large non-metallic dish. Pour over the marinade. Cover and leave to marinate in the refrigerator overnight.
3 Peel, halve and slice the avocados. Add to the scallop mixture with the tomatoes, and toss gently. Spoon on to a large serving platter and garnish with lemon zest, lime slices and herbs before serving. **Serves 6**

SEAFOOD GRATIN

A delicious mixture of moist, succulent flakes of salmon with plump scallops, prawns and fennel. This combination – with its creamed potato topping – makes a perfect buffet lunch dish. I like to serve it with a tomato salad. For a party I prepare it to the end of stage 4 the day before and leave in the refrigerator overnight.

500g (1lb) salmon tail · 155ml (5 fl oz/2/3 cup) dry white wine · 250g (8oz) small queen scallops · 375g (12oz) Florence fennel, thinly sliced · 125g (4oz) peeled prawns · 125g (4oz) butter · 60g (2oz/ 1/2 cup) plain flour · 75ml (2 1/2 fl oz/1/3 cup) single (light) cream · 1 tablespoon chopped dill · salt and pepper to taste · 1 kg (2lb) old potatoes 125ml (4 fl oz/1/2 cup) milk · beaten egg to glaze

To Garnish:
dill sprigs

1 Place the salmon in a saucepan, pour over the wine and 375ml (12 fl oz/1 1/2 cups) water. Bring almost to the boil, cover and simmer very gently until almost tender, about 10-12 minutes. Add the scallops and simmer for 1 minute. Strain the cooking liquor and reserve.

2 Cook the fennel in boiling salted water for 12 minutes; drain.

3 Skin and bone the salmon, then flake into a 1.75 litre (3 pint) large ovenproof dish. Scatter the scallops, prawns and fennel on top.

4 Melt half the butter in a saucepan. Add the flour and cook, stirring, for 1 minute. Stir in the reserved liquor. Bring to the boil, stirring, and simmer for 1 minute. Off the heat, beat in the cream, dill and seasoning. Pour over the fish.

5 Preheat the oven to 190C (375F/Gas 5). Cook the potatoes in boiling salted water until tender; drain and mash. Beat in the milk, remaining butter and seasoning. Spoon or pipe the potatoes over the fish. Brush lightly with egg.

6 Bake for 35-40 minutes or until golden brown and hot through. Garnish with dill sprigs. **Serves 8**

CRAB RAVIOLI WITH CHIVE SAUCE

A cheat's method of making 'ravioli' – but very successful. If preferred, you can use lobster tails or prawns instead of crab. If time, try making your own pasta – rolling it out very thinly.

4 sheets fresh lasagne

Crab Filling:
375g (12oz) fresh mixed crab meat (or frozen and thawed) · 5 tablespoons double (thick) cream pinch of ground ginger · pinch of ground mace salt and pepper to taste

Chive Butter Sauce:
1 shallot, finely chopped · 3 tablespoons (9 tsp) white wine vinegar · 250g (8oz) unsalted butter, chilled and cubed · squeeze of lemon juice 2 tablespoons chopped chives

To Garnish:
few chives

1 To make the crab filling, in a small pan, mix together the crab, cream, spices and seasoning. Warm through over a low heat, then keep warm.

2 For the chive butter sauce, put the shallot and vinegar in a small pan with 3 tablespoons water. Boil until reduced to 2 tablespoons. Over a low heat, gradually whisk in the butter, a piece at a time, until creamy and amalgamated; this process shouldn't take too long. Do not allow to boil or the sauce will separate. Season with salt and pepper and stir in the lemon juice and chives. Keep warm in a bowl, placed over a pan of hot water.

3 Cut each lasagne sheet in half to give 8 large squares. Cook in plenty of boiling salted water, according to the manufacturer's instructions, until *al dente* (cooked but still firm to the bite). Drain and toss in a little of the sauce.

4 Place a pasta square on each of 4 warmed serving plates. Divide the crab filling between them and top with the remaining pasta squares. Spoon a little chive butter sauce over the pasta and garnish with chives. Serve immediately. **Serves 4**

CELEBRATION SALMON

It's difficult to top salmon as a centrepiece for a special occasion buffet. This is definitely the best way of cooking a whole fish to serve cold. It never fails – the flesh is always beautifully moist and never overcooked.
If you haven't got a fish kettle or roasting tin large enough to hold the salmon flat, curl it into a large preserving pan. It will keep the curled shape after cooking and looks just as impressive!

1.75kg (3½lb) salmon or sea trout · 60ml (2 fl oz/ ¼ cup) white wine · ½ onion, sliced · ½ carrot, sliced · few black peppercorns · bay leaf ½ teaspoon powdered gelatine 4 tablespoons chopped dill

To Garnish:
lemon and lime slices · dill and parsley sprigs

1 Place the salmon or sea trout in a fish kettle or large roasting tin. Add the wine, onion, carrot, peppercorns and bay leaf. Pour over just enough cold water to cover the fish completely.
2 Bring just to the boil, then cover tightly with a lid or foil. Simmer very gently for 2 minutes, then turn off the heat and leave the fish in the liquid, still covered, to cool until lukewarm.
3 Carefully lift the warm salmon out of the poaching liquid on to a board. Strain the liquor, reserving 155ml (5 fl oz/⅔ cup). Skin the fish and place on a large oval serving platter. Cover loosely with plastic wrap and place in the refrigerator.
4 Put the reserved liquor in a small bowl, sprinkle on the gelatine and leave to soften for 2-3 minutes. Stand the bowl in a saucepan of hot water and leave until dissolved.
5 Brush a little of this liquid over the cold salmon. Stir the chopped dill into the remaining liquid. Spoon evenly over the fish flesh to cover.
6 Serve the salmon or sea trout garnished with lemon and lime slices, dill and parsley sprigs. **Serves 8-10**

SALMON STEAKS WITH TARRAGON

The attraction of this dish lies in its speed and simplicity. If the medallions are prepared ahead and refrigerated, it takes less than 15 minutes to complete. I prefer to bone the salmon steaks and curl them to form neat medallions, but you can cook them as steaks if you prefer.
Serve with a selection of quick-to-cook vegetables such as fine asparagus, mange tout (snow peas) and new potatoes.

8 salmon steaks, each about 155g (5oz)
155 g (5oz) butter · 8 lime slices · 1 small bunch tarragon · 185ml (6 fl oz/¾ cup) fish stock (preferably salmon stock) · 185ml (6 fl oz/¾ cup) crème fraîche · salt and pepper to taste

1 Preheat the oven to 220C (425F/Gas 7). Carefully remove the centre bone from each salmon steak and halve each steak to form 2 cutlets. Skin and curl these pairs of cutlets around each other to form small medallions. Secure with fine string.
2 Melt half the butter in a frying pan, add the salmon medallions with the lime slices, and brown quickly on both sides.
3 Place each salmon medallion on a 20cm (8 inch) square of greaseproof paper. Add a lime slice, a sprig of tarragon and a little melted butter. Bring up the edges of the paper and twist to enclose the salmon. Tie with string. Cook in the oven for 10-15 minutes until just tender.
4 Meanwhile, add the remaining butter to the pan with the fish stock and crème fraîche. Bring to the boil and simmer for 3-4 minutes. Remove from the heat and add a little chopped tarragon to taste. Adjust the seasoning.
5 To serve, open out the salmon parcels and pour in a little of the cream sauce; serve the remainder separately. Garnish each parcel with a fresh sprig of tarragon. **Serves 8**

FISH STEAKS WITH VEGETABLES

This dish is so easy – fish is braised in wine on a bed of vegetables to add flavour and prevent overcooking. You will need a large enough pan to hold the fish steaks in a single layer.
Serve this delicately flavoured dish with buttered new potatoes or a potato gratin.

60g (2oz) butter · 375g (12oz) small baby carrots, halved lengthwise · 1 fennel bulb, cut into strips 2 small courgettes (zucchini), cut into strips 1 teaspoon finely grated lemon rind · 1 tablespoon chopped parsley · 4 fish steaks, such as cod, salmon or halibut, each weighing 220g (7oz) · salt and pepper · 155ml (5 fl oz/⅔ cup) white or rosé wine

To Garnish:
lemon slices · parsley sprigs

1 Melt the butter in a large shallow pan. Add the carrots and fennel and sauté gently for 3 minutes. Stir in the courgettes (zucchini), lemon rind and parsley.
2 Arrange the fish steaks on top of the vegetables, season with salt and pepper and pour over the wine. Cover tightly and simmer for about 10-12 minutes until the fish is opaque and cooked through; do not allow to overcook.
3 Carefully lift the fish steaks on to warmed serving plates and surround with the vegetables. Spoon the wine juices over the fish and garnish with lemon slices and sprigs of parsley. **Serves 4**

TROUT WITH BACON & ALMONDS

I love to eat grilled trout with french fries – 'glorified fish and chips' – but for a light lunch or dinner a green salad or vegetable and new potatoes are more appropriate accompaniments.

4 trout, cleaned · juice of ½ lemon · salt and pepper to taste · 60g (2oz/½ cup) slivered almonds
3 rashers streaky bacon, diced · 60g (2oz) butter
1 tablespoon chopped parsley or dill

To Garnish:
lemon slices

1 Preheat the grill to medium. Using a sharp knife, make 2 or 3 deep slashes in each side of the trout. Sprinkle with lemon juice, salt and pepper. Cook under the preheated grill for about 5 minutes on each side, until tender.
2 Meanwhile, place the almonds in a non-stick frying pan over moderate heat, shaking the pan constantly until the almonds are evenly browned. Transfer to a plate and set aside. Add the bacon to the pan and cook over a high heat for about 3 minutes until crisp. Add the butter and, while it is sizzling, scrape up any bacon residue with a wooden spoon. Stir in the almonds and parsley or dill.
3 Spoon the bacon and almond mixture over the trout and serve garnished with lemon slices. **Serves 4**

VARIATION: Make a simple stuffing for the trout. Heat 30g (1oz) butter in a small pan and sauté 1 finely chopped leek for 1 minute to soften. Add 2 tablespoons fresh white breadcrumbs, ½ teaspoon grated lemon rind and seasoning to taste. Use to fill the trout cavities before grilling.

MARINATED HALIBUT STEAKS

A simple marinade, but a superb combination of flavours to complement fish. Other fish steaks, such as shark or tuna, would also be suitable. I like to serve this dish with garlic bread and a crisp green salad.

2 or 4 halibut steaks

Marinade:
2 cloves garlic, crushed · 1 teaspoon finely chopped fresh root (green) ginger · 1 tablespoon sesame oil
1 tablespoon soy sauce · 3 tablespoons dry sherry
2 spring onions (green shallots), sliced diagonally

1 Mix all the marinade ingredients together in a bowl.
2 Lay the halibut steaks in a shallow dish and pour over the marinade. Cover and leave to marinate in the refrigerator for 2 hours.
3 Lift the fish steaks out of the marinade and grill or barbecue for 4-6 minutes on each side, depending on the thickness. Serve immediately. **Serves 2 or 4**

GARLIC BREAD: Cream 90g (3oz) butter with 2 crushed garlic cloves and seasoning to taste. Slice a French stick diagonally, without cutting right through so the loaf holds together. Spread both sides of the slices with garlic butter. Wrap in foil and place in a preheated oven at 180C (350F/Gas 4) for 15 minutes. Unwrap and crispen for 2-3 minutes.

BARBECUED FISH WITH FENNEL

This is a wonderful idea for a summer barbecue and there are several varieties of whole fish which are particularly suitable. Grey mullet, red mullet, trout, bream, salmon, grouper and mackerel are all good, but sea bass is, I think, the nicest of all. It needs no adornment – save for a few lemon wedges – but I sometimes serve it with fennel mayonnaise and a cucumber salad. Whole fish do not really benefit from a marinade, but adding herbs – such as fennel, bay, thyme or rosemary – to the fire toward the end of cooking, imparts a wonderful aroma and flavour to the fish. Moistening these herbs first with water gives a more pronounced smokey flavour.

1 sea bass (or grouper), weighing about 1 kg (2lb), gutted · salt and pepper to taste · few fennel sprigs olive oil for brushing

To Serve:
lemon wedges and fennel sprigs · fennel mayonnaise (right), (optional)

1 Scale the fish by scraping from tail to head with the back of a small knife, or ask your fishmonger to do so. Make 3 deep diagonal slashes on each side of the fish to allow the heat to penetrate.
2 Season the inside of the fish and insert fennel sprigs. Brush the outside liberally with oil and season.
3 Lay the fish in a hinged grid and barbecue for 10-15 minutes on each side, brushing with more oil occasionally.
4 Divide into portions and garnish with lemon wedges and fennel. Serve with fennel mayonnaise, crusty bread and a leafy salad or a cucumber salad. **Serves 4**

FENNEL MAYONNAISE: Mix 60ml (2 fl oz/ ¼ cup) each mayonnaise and Greek yogurt with 1 tablespoon chopped fennel and seasoning to taste.

SPICED FISH KEBABS

Any firm fleshed fish can be used for these kebabs: try tuna, monkfish (or kingfish) if you prefer. Unlike whole fish, steaks and cubed fish are improved by marinating. Saffron rice makes a good accompaniment.

500g (1 lb) swordfish or halibut

Marinade:
1 teaspoon tandoori spice mix · 155ml (5 fl oz/ 2/3 cup) natural yogurt · 2 tablespoons sunflower oil juice of 1/2 lemon · 15g (1/2 oz) creamed coconut, blended with 1 tablespoon boiling water

To Serve:
lemon wedges

1 Cut the fish into 2.5cm (1 inch) cubes and put into a shallow dish.
2 Mix all the marinade ingredients together in a bowl until smooth, then pour over the fish. Turn to coat completely and leave to marinate for 2 hours.
3 Lift the fish out of the marinade, thread on to skewers and grill or barbecue for 8-10 minutes, brushing with extra marinade and turning occasionally. Serve with lemon wedges and rice. **Serves 4**

HERBY FISH KEBABS: As an alternative, use a herb marinade. Mix together 3 tablespoons olive oil, 3 tablespoons lemon juice and 1 tablespoon chopped herbs, such as parsley, thyme, dill or fennel. Season to taste. Marinate fish for 2 hours, then thread onto skewers interspersing with bay leaves. Cook as above.

BARBECUED FISH STEAKS: Buy thick steaks, or they will dry out over the barbecue. Cover with the marinade, leave for 2 hours, then cook for 10-15 minutes, turning once.

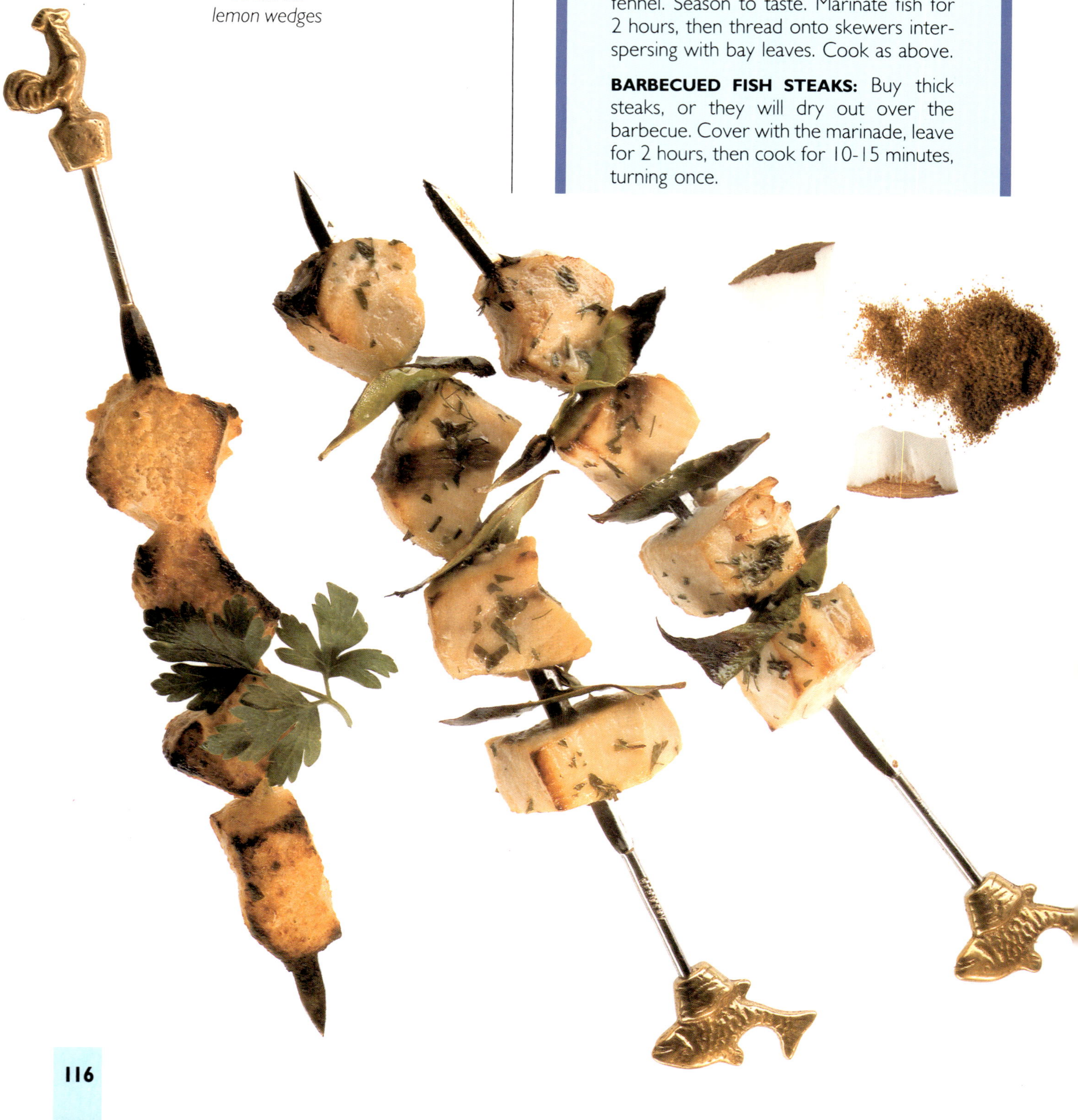

SCALLOP & BACON KEBABS

Bacon-wrapped scallops are delicious grilled or cooked on the barbecue. The delicate scallop flesh is protected, remaining succulent inside the crisp bacon. Being fairly quick to cook they are ideal to serve while waiting for other barbecued foods. If serving as a main course, accompany with rice.

12 scallops, halved
12 rashers streaky bacon, rinds removed

Marinade:
1 clove garlic, finely chopped · 1 tablespoon chopped fennel · 2 tablespoons olive oil
1 tablespoon lemon juice

Fennel Mayonnaise:
60ml (2 fl oz/¼ cup) mayonnaise · 60ml (2 fl oz/¼ cup) natural yogurt · 1 tablespoon chopped fennel · 1 tablespoon Pernod (optional)
salt and pepper to taste

1 To make the marinade, mix the garlic, fennel, oil and lemon juice together in a bowl. Add the scallops to the marinade, mix well and leave for 30 minutes.
2 Stretch the bacon with the back of a knife until thin, then cut each rasher in half.
3 Lift the scallops from the marinade and wrap each one in a piece of bacon. Thread on to 4 long skewers.
4 To make the mayonnaise, mix all the ingredients together in a bowl.
5 Grill or barbecue the kebabs for 8-10 minutes, turning occasionally. Serve immediately, with the fennel mayonnaise. **Serves 4**

SALMON BROCHETTES: In place of the bacon-wrapped scallops, use 375g (12oz) each salmon and monkfish (or kingfish). Cut into 2.5cm (1 inch) squares and marinate (as above) in the refrigerator for 2 hours. Thread on to wooden skewers and cook as above.

MEAT & POULTRY

An exciting collection of main course dishes with an emphasis on cooking lean cuts of meat with fresh vegetables and herbs. Most of the recipes are very easy to prepare and fast and simple to cook. Choose from tasty stir-fries, grilled and barbecued meat dishes, tempting bakes and sustaining casseroles.

COCONUT CREAM CHICKEN

Don't be put off by the inclusion of green chilli in this dish; the sauce is very mild and creamy. Slice the chicken before serving if you want to serve it as fork food. Rice is an ideal accompaniment.

4 tablespoons oil · 1.5kg (3lb) boneless chicken 125g (4oz) onion, finely chopped · 1 clove garlic, crushed · 1 teaspoon each ground coriander, turmeric, paprika, mild curry powder and poppy seeds · 60g (2oz) creamed coconut, grated 1-2 green chillis, finely sliced · 185g (6oz) tomatoes, skinned, seeded and chopped 90ml (3 fl oz/⅓ cup) double (thick) cream salt and pepper to taste

To Garnish:
lime slices · coriander sprigs

1 Heat the oil in a large sauté pan, add the chicken and brown evenly; remove and set aside. Add the onion and garlic to the pan and cook, stirring, for 1-2 minutes. Stir in the spices, creamed coconut and chilli(s). Cook, stirring, for 1 minute.

2 Stir in the tomatoes, chicken and 250ml (8 fl oz/1 cup) water. Bring to the boil, cover and simmer for about 25 minutes.

3 Stir in the cream and simmer for 1-2 minutes; adjust the seasoning. Garnish with lime slices and coriander sprigs to serve. **Serves 8**

LEMON GINGER CHICKEN

This tasty dish of chicken fillets steeped in lemon juice and topped with a crispy sugar coating is one of my favourites. It works well with duck breast too. Serve with a leafy salad.

750g (1 ½lb) chicken breast fillets · 220ml (7 fl oz/ ⅞ cup) lemon juice · 2 cloves garlic, crushed 2.5cm (1 inch) piece fresh root (green) ginger, sliced 1 stalk lemon grass (optional) · 60ml (2 fl oz/ ¼ cup) grapeseed oil · 90ml (3 fl oz/⅓ cup) chicken stock · 60g (2 oz/⅓ cup) soft brown sugar

Lemon Mayonnaise:
75ml (2½ fl oz/⅓ cup) mayonnaise
155ml (5 fl oz/⅔ cup) thick sour cream
60ml (2 fl oz/¼ cup) milk · salt and pepper to taste
grated rind of 1 lemon

To Garnish:
lemon wedges · coriander or parsley sprigs

1 Place the chicken, lemon juice, garlic, ginger and lemon grass if using, in a large non-metallic bowl. Mix well, cover and leave to marinate in the refrigerator overnight.

2 Drain the chicken, reserving the marinade. Heat half the oil in a large non-stick frying pan and brown the chicken a few pieces at a time, adding more oil as necessary.

3 Return all the chicken to the pan, and add the marinade and stock. Simmer, uncovered, for 10-12 minutes until the chicken is tender. Remove from the heat and leave to cool in the liquid.

4 Preheat the grill to high. Drain the chicken pieces and place in the grill pan. Sprinkle with the sugar and grill for a few minutes on each side until crisp and golden.

5 In a small bowl, mix together the mayonnaise, sour cream, milk, seasoning and lemon rind. Serve the warm chicken on a bed of rice salad, accompanied by the lemon mayonnaise. **Serves 8**

THAI CHICKEN WITH BASIL

A friend recently returned from Thailand raving about a delicious chicken and basil dish she had consumed large quantities of. I saw the simple idea as a perfect fast supper dish and promptly stole it for inclusion here! It is particularly good served with egg fried rice.

4 boneless chicken breasts, skinned · 4 tablespoons groundnut or olive oil · 2 cloves garlic, crushed 2 red chillies, sliced · 2 tablespoons light soy sauce at least 45g (1 ½oz) basil leaves · salt and pepper

To Garnish:
basil sprigs

1 Cut the chicken into long strips, about 5mm (¼ inch) thick.

2 Heat the oil in a wok or large frying pan. Add the garlic and chillies and cook, stirring for 1 minute, without browning. Add the chicken strips and stir-fry over a high heat for 4-5 minutes until cooked through. Stir in the soy sauce.

3 Stir in the basil leaves just before serving and heat through. Season with salt and pepper to taste. Serve immediately, garnished with basil sprigs and accompanied by egg fried rice.

Serves 4

VARIATION: Replace the soy sauce with ½ lemon, sliced, plus the juice of ½ lemon and 1 teaspoon soft brown sugar. Stir-fry for a further 1-2 minutes before adding the basil leaves.

HOT CHICKEN SALAD WITH MANGO

Medallions of chicken, crisp mange tout (snow peas), cashews and ripe mango make a delicious combination – especially mingled with the flavours of sesame, lime and coriander. Be sure to use a mango that is ripe, golden and scented.

125g (4oz) mange tout (snow peas) · 1 ripe mango 60g (2oz/⅓ cup) salted cashews · 3 skinned chicken breast fillets · 1½ tablespoons sesame oil 5 tablespoons groundnut oil · ½ clove garlic, crushed · 2 tablespoons sherry vinegar · grated rind and juice of ½ lime · pinch of sugar · pepper to taste · handful of coriander leaves

To Garnish:
1½ tablespoons toasted sesame seeds

1 Top and tail the mange tout (snow peas). Blanch in boiling water for a few seconds then refresh in cold water and drain. Peel the mango, cut the flesh away from the stone and slice thinly. Place in a salad bowl with the mange tout (snow peas) and cashews.

2 Cut the chicken breasts crosswise into thick slices and, using a rolling pin, flatten the slices between two sheets of greaseproof paper or plastic wrap to give thin 'medallions'.

3 Heat the sesame oil and 2 tablespoons groundnut oil in a large frying pan. Add the chicken pieces, a few at a time, and sauté for 2-3 minutes, turning once, until lightly browned and cooked right through. Transfer to a plate and keep warm until all the pieces are cooked.

4 Add the remaining oil to the pan with the garlic, sherry vinegar, lime juice and sugar. Season with pepper to taste and heat gently.

5 Add the chicken pieces to the salad with the lime rind and coriander leaves. Spoon over the dressing and toss gently to mix. Serve immediately, sprinkled with toasted sesame seeds. **Serves 4**

CHICKEN SATÉ

Originating from Indonesia, satés are cubes of meat or fish, threaded on to sticks and traditionally cooked over charcoal. Any type of lean, tender meat or fish can be used. Peanut sauce is the usual accompaniment: if you prefer, replace the peanuts with crunchy peanut butter.

4 boneless chicken breasts, skinned

Marinade:

4 tablespoons soy sauce · 2 cloves garlic, crushed
2 tablespoons lemon juice · 1 tablespoon sesame oil
1 tablespoon clear honey

Peanut Sauce:

2 tablespoons sunflower oil · 1 onion, chopped
2 cloves garlic, chopped · ½ teaspoon chilli powder
1 teaspoon ground cumin · 1 teaspoon ground coriander · 1 teaspoon paprika · 185ml (6 fl oz/ ¾ cup) water · 125g (4oz/¾ cup) shelled peanuts, finely ground

1 Cut the chicken into 2.5cm (1 inch) cubes and put into a shallow dish.

2 Mix all the marinade ingredients together in a bowl, then pour over the chicken, stir well to coat and leave to marinate for 2 hours.

3 Meanwhile make the peanut sauce. Heat the oil in a pan, add the onion and fry gently until softened. Add the garlic and spices and fry gently for 1 minute, then add the water. Stir in the ground peanuts, bring to the boil and cook, stirring, for 2 minutes. Remove from the heat.

4 Lift the chicken pieces out of the marinade and thread on to saté sticks. Add three quarters of the remaining marinade to the peanut sauce and thin with a little water if necessary. Reheat, then keep warm while cooking the saté.

5 Grill or barbecue the saté for 4-5 minutes on each side, brushing frequently with the remaining marinade. Serve with the peanut sauce and rice. **Serves 4**

CHICKEN TIKKA

I particularly like chicken cooked this way, but other meats are also good – notably lamb. A firm fleshed fish, such as halibut or swordfish, will also give excellent results. Naan bread, lemon wedges and an onion salad make ideal accompaniments.

4 boneless chicken breasts, about 625g (1 1/4lb) total weight

Marinade:

3 cloves garlic, crushed · 1 cm (1/2 inch) piece fresh root (green) ginger, peeled and crushed 2 teaspoons ground coriander · 1 teaspoon ground cinnamon · 1 teaspoon ground cumin · 1 teaspoon turmeric · 1 tablespoon paprika · 1/4 teaspoon chilli powder · 1/2 teaspoon salt · 155ml (5 fl oz/2/3 cup) natural yogurt · 2 tablespoons sunflower oil juice of 1/2 lemon

To Serve:

lemon wedges

1 To make the marinade, mix the garlic, ginger, spices and salt together in a shallow dish. Add the yogurt, oil and lemon juice and mix well.

2 Cut the chicken into 2.5cm (1 inch) cubes, add to the marinade and turn to coat completely. Leave for about 2 hours.

3 Lift the pieces of chicken out of the marinade and thread on to skewers. Grill or barbecue for 8-10 minutes, turning and brushing with more marinade occasionally. Serve with lemon wedges, warm naan bread and an onion salad (below). **Serves 4**

ONION SALAD: Slice 2 onions into thin rings, sprinkle with 4 tablespoons wine vinegar and 2 tablespoons chopped coriander leaves. Marinate for 30 minutes, turning occasionally.

SMOKED CHICKEN LASAGNE

This delicious rich creamy dish can be assembled the day before, ready to cook when required. Serve with a crisp green salad and warm French bread. Don't be put off by the vast amount of sauce in this recipe – the pasta absorbs it during cooking!

185g (6oz) butter · 500g (1lb) brown cap mushrooms, sliced · 2 tablespoons lemon juice · salt and pepper to taste · 125g (4oz/1 cup) plain flour 1 litre (1¾ pints/4 cups) milk · 1 litre (1¾ pints/ 4 cups) chicken stock · 142g (5oz) packet full-fat soft cheese with herbs · 90g (3oz) gruyère cheese, grated · 1 clove garlic, crushed · 250g (8oz) frozen chopped spinach, thawed · 1kg (2 lb) boneless poached chicken, skinned · 250g (8oz) boneless smoked chicken, skinned · 315g (10oz) quick-cook egg lasagne · 60g (2oz/1 cup) fresh white breadcrumbs

To Garnish:
few chives

1 Preheat the oven to 200C (400F/Gas 6). Melt 60g (2oz) butter in a large saucepan. Add the mushrooms, lemon juice and seasoning. Cook, stirring, for 3-4 minutes, then remove the mushrooms with a slotted spoon and set aside.

2 Simmer the pan juices until reduced by about half, then add the remaining butter and heat until melted. Add the flour and cook, stirring, for 1 minute. Stir in the milk and stock, bring to the boil and simmer, stirring, for 1-2 minutes. Remove from the heat and beat in the soft cheese, gruyére, garlic, spinach and seasoning.

3 Cut both types of chicken into bite-sized pieces and mix together. Spoon a little of the sauce into one large, or two medium ovenproof dishes. Cover with a layer of lasagne, followed by chicken, mushrooms and sauce. Continue layering in this way, finishing with a layer of sauce. Sprinkle the breadcrumbs over the top.

4 Bake for 1-1¼ hours until golden and hot through. Garnish with chives to serve.

Serves 8-10

CHICKEN & MOZZARELLA GRATIN

This is an excellent dish to serve at a party and is easily doubled up, I'd serve a basket of hot garlic and herb bread, and a large mixed salad with it. Slice the chicken before cooking if your guests will be eating standing up.

1kg (2lb) aubergines (eggplants) · about 4 tablespoons oil · 750g (1½lb) boneless chicken breasts, skinned · 1 egg, beaten · 90g (3oz/¾ cup) freshly grated Parmesan cheese · 1 clove garlic, crushed · 250g (8oz) onion, finely chopped · 400g (14oz) can chopped tomatoes · 2 teaspoons dried mixed herbs · pinch of sugar · salt and pepper to taste · 220g (7oz) mozzarella cheese, sliced

1 Preheat the oven to 190C (375F/Gas 5). Thickly slice the aubergines (eggplants). Cook in boiling salted water for 2-3 minutes or until just beginning to soften. Drain and refresh under cold water. Dry on absorbent kitchen paper.

2 Preheat the grill to high. Brush the aubergine (eggplant) slices lightly with oil and grill on both sides until lightly browned.

3 Dip the chicken into the beaten egg, then into the Parmesan cheese to coat. Heat 2 tablespoons oil in a large sauté pan, add the chicken and sauté until evenly browned; remove and set aside.

4 Heat a further 1 tablespoon oil in the sauté pan. Add the garlic and onion and cook, stirring, for 1-2 minutes, then stir in the tomatoes, mixed herbs, sugar and seasoning.

5 Spoon the sauce into a large, shallow ovenproof dish. Arrange overlapping rows of chicken, aubergine (eggplant) and mozzarella on top of the tomato sauce. Sprinkle with any remaining Parmesan cheese.

6 Bake, uncovered for 35-40 minutes or until golden brown and cooked through. **Serves 6**

STIR-FRIED TURKEY WITH COURGETTES

I usually serve this on a bed of hot egg noodles or pasta tossed in olive oil, lemon juice and coarsely ground black pepper.

1kg (2lb) turkey fillets, cut into bite-sized pieces

Marinade:

2 teaspoons caster sugar · 1 teaspoon ground ginger · 1 teaspoon turmeric · 1 teaspoon curry powder · 1 teaspoon chilli seasoning 1 teaspoon milk

Stir-fry:

60ml (2 fl oz/¼ cup) grapeseed oil · 500g (1lb) courgettes (zucchini), thinly sliced · 375g (12oz) sugar snap peas · 2 red peppers, cored, seeded and cut into strips · 60g (2oz/⅓ cup) cashew nuts 75ml (2½ fl oz/⅓ cup) lemon juice 60ml (2 fl oz/¼ cup) clear honey

1 First combine the ingredients for the marinade in a shallow dish. Add the turkey, toss well, cover and leave to marinate in a cool place overnight.

2 Heat half the oil in a large sauté pan or frying pan, add the courgettes (zucchini), sugar snap peas and red peppers and sauté for 3-4 minutes. Transfer to a large bowl.

3 Heat the remaining oil in the pan and sauté the turkey pieces, a few at a time, until golden. Return all the turkey to the pan and add the cashew nuts, lemon juice and honey.

4 Cook, stirring for a further 3-4 minutes or until the turkey is tender. Return the vegetables to the pan and heat through, stirring. Serve on a bed of egg noodles if you like. **Serves 8**

VARIATION: Instead of returning the vegetables to the pan to heat through, add the cooked turkey to them. Allow to cool before serving, with the hot noodles.

DUCK BREAST WITH ROQUETTE & ORANGE

Succulent breast of duck, with tangy orange slices, roquette and ribbons of courgettes (zucchini), makes an elegant main course salad. You can cook the duck and prepare the dressing ahead, leaving little last minute preparation. Serve with new potatoes.

4 boneless duck breasts · 2 teaspoons sesame oil
1 tablespoon olive oil · 2 courgettes (zucchini)
2 oranges · about 60g (2oz) roquette

Dressing:
4 tablespoons olive oil · 1 tablespoon sesame oil
2 tablespoons red wine vinegar · 2 teaspoons finely chopped parsley · 1 teaspoon grated orange rind
pinch of sugar · salt and pepper to taste

To Garnish:
2 teaspoons toasted sesame seeds

1 Using a sharp knife make 3 or 4 diagonal slashes in the skin of each duck breast. Heat the oils in a large frying pan, add the duck breasts and cook over a fairly high heat for 5-7 minutes, turning once, until well browned on the outside and just pink within. Transfer to a plate and leave to cool.

2 To make the dressing, stir all the ingredients together in a small bowl or shake in a screw-top jar to combine.

3 Using a potato peeler, pare the courgettes (zucchini) into long thin 'ribbons'. Peel the oranges, removing all the pith, and slice thinly.

4 Arrange the courgettes (zucchini), orange slices and roquette on individual serving plates. Slice each duck breast and arrange in a fan shape on each plate. Spoon the dressing over the salads and serve immediately, sprinkled with toasted sesame seeds. **Serves 4**

VARIATION: Prepare the dressing, courgettes and orange before cooking the duck. Serve the duck warm, with the salad.

DUCKLING & CASHEW NUT PILAF

Most supermarkets now sell duckling breasts but if you prefer, use chicken breast fillets instead. Slice the duckling before serving if you wish.

75ml (2½ fl oz/⅓ cup) olive oil · 1kg (2lb) boneless duckling breasts, halved · 90g (3oz/⅔ cup) cashew nuts · 375g (12oz) onion, chopped 1 green chilli, seeded and finely chopped 4 teaspoons ground coriander · 2 cloves garlic, crushed · 690ml (22 fl oz/2¾ cups) chicken stock 625ml (1 pint/2½ cups) dry cider · salt and pepper to taste · 500g (1lb/3 cups) long-grain white rice 3 tablespoons chopped parsley

To Garnish:
lemon slices · parsley sprigs

1 Preheat the oven to 160C (325F/Gas 3). Heat the oil in a large flameproof casserole. Add the duck pieces a few at a time with the cashew nuts and fry gently until a deep golden brown. Remove with a slotted spoon and set aside.

2 Add the onion to the casserole and cook, stirring, for 1-2 minutes. Add the chilli, coriander and garlic. Cook, stirring, for 1 minute. Add the stock, cider and seasoning. Bring to the boil.

3 Return all the duck pieces and cashew nuts to the pan. Cover tightly and cook in the oven for 45 minutes. Stir in the rice, re-cover and return to the oven for a further 35 minutes or until the rice is tender and most of the liquid absorbed. Stir in the chopped parsley and adjust the seasoning. Serve garnished with lemon slices and parsley sprigs. **Serves 6**

STIR-FRIED DUCK WITH CUCUMBER

The richness of the duck is balanced by the delicate flavour of the cucumber in this stir-fry. Don't overcook the cucumber or the texture will be totally lost. Serve with plain boiled rice.

500g (1 lb) duck breasts, skinned and thinly sliced
1 clove garlic, crushed · 2.5cm (1 inch) piece fresh root (green) ginger, grated · 4 tablespoons dry sherry · 1 teaspoon cornflour · pinch of sugar
3 tablespoons soy sauce · 90ml (3 fl oz/⅓ cup) chicken stock or water · ½ cucumber
3 tablespoons oil · 1 small red pepper, cut into strips
3 spring onions (green shallots), chopped

To Garnish:
coriander sprigs

1 Place the duck in a shallow dish. Add the garlic, ginger and sherry, stir and leave to marinate for at least 1 hour.

2 In another bowl, mix together the cornflour, sugar, soy sauce and stock or water. Set aside.

3 Using a canelle knife, remove and discard strips of peel along the length of the cucumber. Cut in half lengthwise and scoop out the seeds. Cut the flesh into 5mm (¼ inch) slices.

4 Heat the oil in a large frying pan or wok. Add the duck mixture and stir-fry over high heat for 3 minutes. Add the red pepper and spring onions (shallots) and stir-fry for 2 minutes. Stir in the cornflour mixture and cook until thickened. Add the cucumber and stir-fry briefly for about 30 seconds until just heated through.

5 Serve immediately, garnished with coriander and accompanied by plain boiled rice. **Serves 4**

VARIATION: Replace the duck breast with fillet of lamb and garnish with a little chopped mint.

MADEIRA PORK WITH MANGE TOUT

Slices of pork tenderloin and crisp mange tout (snow peas) are cooked with garlic and flavoured with a delicious Madeira and cream sauce. Serve with new potatoes or pasta.

2 tablespoons oil · 185g (6oz) mange tout (snow peas), topped and tailed · 30g (1 oz) butter 500g (1 lb) pork tenderloin, sliced · 1 shallot, finely chopped · 2 cloves garlic, sliced · 125ml (4 fl oz/ ½ cup) Madeira · 4 tablespoons double (thick) cream · salt and pepper

To Garnish:
parsley or chervil sprigs

1 Heat 1 tablespoon oil in a large frying pan or wok. Add the mange tout (snow peas) and stir-fry for 1 minute. Transfer to a plate and set aside.
2 Add the remaining oil and the butter to the pan, heat until sizzling, then add the pork, shallot and garlic. Stir-fry for 3 minutes until the pork is sealed on all sides.
3 Add the Madeira to the pan and cook over a high heat for 2-3 minutes until the juices are slightly reduced. Stir in the cream and mange tout (snow peas) and heat through gently. Season with salt and pepper to taste.
4 Serve immediately, garnished with parsley or chervil sprigs.
Serves 4

CHICKEN IN WHITE WINE WITH MANGE TOUT: Replace the pork with 500g (1lb) chicken breast fillets, sliced. Use a dry white wine instead of Madeira.

PORK STUFFED WITH PROSCIUTTO

Pork tenderloin is stuffed with prosciutto and sage, then roasted and sliced, to give pretty 'cartwheels' of delicious tender meat. Marsala wine cooking juices provide a good, rich dressing. This dish is excellent served with new potatoes.

375g (12oz) pork tenderloin · 90g (3oz) prosciutto, shredded · 15g (½oz) sage leaves, shredded 4 tablespoons olive oil · 155ml (5 fl oz/⅔ cup) Marsala · salt and pepper to taste · ½ head lollo rosso or mignonette lettuce · about 185g (6oz) young spinach leaves · 1 red onion, thinly sliced

1 Make a deep cut along the length of the pork tenderloin and open out to give a rectangle shape. Cut again along each half, taking care not to slice right through. Beat gently with a rolling pin to flatten the meat further and even out the shape.

2 Arrange the prosciutto and sage in a layer over the meat, roll up from the longest side and secure with string to give a long, neat sausage shape.

3 Preheat the oven to 220C (425F/Gas 7). Heat the oil in a large frying pan. Add the meat and cook over a high heat for 2 minutes, turning to brown and seal on all sides. Transfer the meat and juices to a small roasting dish. Pour over the Marsala and bake in the preheated oven for 15 minutes, turning the meat halfway through the cooking time.

4 Remove the meat from the roasting dish and strain the cooking juices into a small bowl. Season with salt and pepper to taste.

5 Arrange the lollo rosso or mignonette, spinach and onion on a serving platter or individual plates. Slice the stuffed pork fillet and arrange alongside the salad. Spoon the warm cooking juices over and serve immediately.

Serves 4

SAUSAGE & POTATO SKEWERS

For these I usually buy homemade spicy pork sausages from my local Italian delicatessen, or choose a good quality pork sausage from the butcher or supermarket.
Serve with hot pitta bread and a side salad, such as cherry tomato and bean salad (page 74).

12 button onions, peeled · 12 small new potatoes
750g (1 ½lb) coarse pork sausages

Marinade:
315ml (10 fl oz/1 ¼ cups) Greek strained yogurt
pinch of turmeric · 1 tablespoon chopped mint
3 tablespoons olive oil · 2 tablespoons honey
salt and pepper to taste

To Serve:
small mint leaves · shredded spring onion (green shallot) · pitta bread

1 Simmer the button onions and new potatoes in salted water until almost tender, about 5 minutes. Drain well. Cut each sausage into 4cm (1 ½ inch) lengths.
2 Beat together the marinade ingredients. Add the sausage pieces, onions and potatoes. Stir well, cover and refrigerate overnight.
3 Preheat the grill or barbecue to high. Remove the sausage, onions and potatoes from the marinade with a slotted spoon. Strain the marinade and reserve. Thread the sausage, onions and potatoes alternately on to small wooden skewers. Grill or barbecue for 7-10 minutes, turning occasionally and basting frequently with the marinade.
4 Serve the skewers sprinkled with mint leaves and accompanied by shredded spring onion (shallot) and hot pitta bread.

Serves 6

MIDDLE EASTERN LAMB KEBABS

Tasty long rissoles of spiced minced lamb are grilled on skewers and served with a light yogurt sauce. Use lean ground beef in place of lamb if you prefer.

Kebabs:

500g (1 lb) lean minced lamb · ½ onion, grated · 1 clove garlic, crushed · 1 tablespoon tomato purée (paste) · 2 teaspoons flour · 1 tablespoon chopped coriander leaves · juice of ½ lime · ½ teaspoon ground coriander · ½ teaspoon ground cumin · ½ teaspoon chilli powder · salt and pepper to taste

Sauce:

155ml (5 fl oz/⅔ cup) thick yogurt · 1 clove garlic, crushed · 1 tablespoon chopped mint

To Serve:

1 cos lettuce heart, shredded · 1 red onion, thinly sliced · 4 lime slices, halved · coriander or parsley sprigs to garnish

1 Put all the ingredients for the kebabs in a bowl and mix thoroughly, using your hands, until smooth and evenly blended. Divide the mixture into 4 portions and carefully shape each portion around a long skewer to make 4 long rissoles. Chill for 1 hour until firm.

2 Meanwhile, prepare the sauce. Mix together the yogurt, garlic and mint in a small bowl and set aside.

3 Preheat the grill to medium hot. Cook the kebabs under the preheated grill, turning frequently, for about 15 minutes, until well browned and cooked right through.

4 Arrange the lettuce, onion and lime slices on individual serving plates. Place a kebab on each plate and spoon over the sauce. Serve immediately, garnished with coriander or parsley.

Serves 4

HONEYED LAMB TAGINE

I find this lamb dish freezes very well. Leave it to thaw overnight at cool room temperature, then simply bring to a simmer for about 20 minutes before serving. A large bowl of steaming hot couscous, subtly flavoured with toasted almonds and pared lemon rind, is the perfect accompaniment.

2 thin-skinned lemons · 5 tablespoons grapeseed oil 185g (6oz) onion, chopped · 2 teaspoons honey 2 cloves garlic, crushed · 2 teaspoons ground allspice · 1 teaspoon ground cinnamon · pinch of chilli powder · 1 litre (1¾ pints/4 cups) lamb stock 2 tablespoons tomato purée (paste) · salt and pepper to taste · 1.5kg (3lb) boned leg of lamb, cubed · 60g (2oz/½ cup) plain flour · 4 firm pears 16 fresh dates, pitted

To Garnish:
pared lemon zest

1 Preheat the oven to 160C (325F/Gas 3). Put the lemons in a saucepan, cover with cold water and bring to the boil. Cover and simmer for 10-12 minutes until softened; drain. Cut each lemon into 6 wedges.

2 Heat the oil in a frying pan, add the onion and honey and cook, stirring, over a low heat until soft and golden. Stir in the garlic, allspice, cinnamon and chilli powder. Cook, stirring, for 1 minute. Spoon into a deep casserole and add the stock, tomato purée (paste) and seasoning.

3 Toss the lamb in the seasoned flour and shake off any excess. Stir the lamb into the onion mixture with the lemon wedges. Cover and cook in the oven for 45 minutes.

4 Peel, quarter and core the pears and stir into the casserole with the dates. Add a little extra stock at this stage if the juices look too thick. Cover and return to the oven for a further 30-40 minutes or until the lamb is very tender.

5 Serve with plenty of steamed couscous and garnish with lemon zest.

Serves 8

YOGURTLU KEBAB

A really tasty Turkish dish of grilled or barbecued lamb, served on crisp slices of pitta, topped with tomato sauce, creamy yogurt and chopped parsley. If you are barbecuing the kebabs warm the pitta breads through on the barbecue.

750g (1½lb) boned leg of lamb, cut into large cubes · salt and pepper to taste · 2 red peppers, seeded and cut into large squares · 4 pitta breads 155ml (5 fl oz/⅔ cup) Greek yogurt · 4 tablespoons chopped parsley

Marinade:

4 tablespoons olive oil · 2 cloves garlic, crushed juice of ½ lemon

Tomato Sauce:

2 tablespoons olive oil · 1 clove garlic, crushed 500g (1lb) tomatoes, skinned and chopped

1 Mix the marinade ingredients together in a shallow dish, add the seasoned lamb chunks and turn until evenly coated. Leave to marinate for 2 hours.

2 To make the tomato sauce, heat the oil in a pan, add the garlic and fry for 1 minute, then add the tomatoes with seasoning. Cook for 5 minutes; set aside.

3 Remove the meat from the marinade and thread on to skewers, alternately with the red pepper squares.

4 Brush the kebabs with marinade and grill or barbecue for 10-12 minutes, turning and brushing with marinade as they cook.

5 Reheat the tomato sauce and warm the pitta breads through.

6 Slice the pitta and place on the serving dish. Remove the lamb from the skewers and put on top of the pitta. Pour over the tomato sauce, swirl on the yogurt and top with chopped parsley. **Serves 4**

SHISH KEBAB: Marinate the lamb as above, then thread onto skewers interspersing with red and green pepper squares, and onion wedges. Cook as above. Serve with pitta bread and a tomato salad.

MARINATED LAMB CUTLETS

Serve these cutlets with minted new potatoes and a crisp salad for a perfect meal with a light, summery feel.

8 lamb cutlets

Marinade:
75ml (2½ fl oz/⅓ cup) natural yogurt
2 tablespoons olive oil · juice and grated rind of ½ lemon · 1 tablespoon clear honey · ½ clove garlic, crushed · 2 teaspoons fennel seeds, lightly crushed

To Garnish:
lemon slices · mint sprigs

1 Mix all the marinade ingredients together in a small bowl. Place the lamb cutlets in a shallow dish and pour the marinade over. Chill for at least 1 hour.

2 Preheat the grill. Remove the cutlets from the marinade and grill for 6-8 minutes, turning and brushing frequently with marinade. Serve immediately, garnished with lemon slices and mint. **Serves 4**

FILLET STEAKS WITH ROQUEFORT

A quickly prepared special occasion meal, served with a crisp salad of frisée (curly endive) and radicchio leaves.

125g (4oz) Roquefort cheese · 30g (1oz) butter, softened · 2 teaspoons wholegrain mustard ½ teaspoon grated lemon rind · ½ clove garlic, crushed · 1 teaspoon chopped parsley 1 teaspoon chopped chives · 4 fillet steaks, each 2.5cm (1 inch) thick · salt and pepper to taste

To Garnish:
parsley sprigs

1 Using a blender or food processor, blend together the Roquefort, butter, mustard, lemon rind and garlic until smooth. Stir in the herbs and set aside.

2 Preheat the grill. Season the steaks with salt and pepper and grill for 6-10 minutes, according to preference, turning once or twice.

3 Spoon the cheese mixture on top of the steaks and serve immediately, garnished with parsley. **Serves 4**

STEAK WITH GRUYÈRE

Charred steak with a tasty cheese filling, which melts deliciously if the steak is well done. A summer herb salad (page 72) makes an ideal accompaniment.

750g (1½lb) piece rump steak or 2 sirloin steaks, about 4cm (1½ inches) thick · salt and pepper to taste · 90g (3oz) gruyère cheese, grated 1 tablespoon coarse-grain mustard · 2 cloves garlic, crushed · 2 tablespoons olive oil · 2 tablespoons red wine · few thyme sprigs

1 Make a horizontal slit through the lean edge of the steak to make a pocket, then season inside.

2 Mix the gruyère, mustard and 1 clove garlic together in a bowl, then use to fill the pocket and sew up, using fine cotton string.

3 For the marinade, mix the oil, wine, thyme and remaining garlic together in a shallow dish. Add the steak and spoon over the marinade. Leave for 2 hours.

4 Lift the steak out of the marinade. Grill or barbecue, basting occasionally with the marinade, for 5-10 minutes each side, depending how you like your steak cooked. To serve, cut the steak into 1cm (½ inch) slices and accompany with a salad. **Serves 4**

BEEF EN CROÛTE WITH TAPENADE

This is a much lighter version of the traditional beef en croûte. I flavoured mine with tapenade which is a delicious olive paste quite widely available now, both in delicatessens and major supermarkets. You can of course omit the tapenade if you prefer.

Serve with glazed turnips and sautéed mushrooms, or green vegetables, such as broccoli and broad beans, and a gratin of potatoes.

2 tablespoons oil · 1 kg (2lb) piece middle cut fillet of beef · 60g (2oz/⅓ cup) tapenade · 4 large sheets filo pastry · 90g (3oz) butter, melted · salt 1 tablespoon coarse-ground black pepper 142ml (5 fl oz/⅔ cup) thick soured cream

To Garnish:
rosemary sprigs

1 Preheat the oven to 220C (425F/Gas 7). Heat the oil in a frying pan, then add the meat and brown quickly on all sides. Remove and leave to cool and drain on absorbent kitchen paper.

2 Set aside 1 tablespoon tapenade for the tapenade cream. Place a sheet of filo pastry on the work surface and brush lightly with melted butter. Spread with 1 tablespoon tapenade and place another sheet of filo on top. Continue layering the filo, melted butter and tapenade in this way, finishing with tapenade.

3 Place the fillet of beef on top, season and fold the filo pastry over the beef to enclose. Trim off any excess pastry. Place the croûte, seam side down, on a baking sheet. Decorate with leaves cut from the pastry trimmings. Brush with the remaining melted butter. Sprinkle with the black pepper.

4 Bake for 30 minutes, covering lightly with foil if the pastry appears to be browning too quickly. The meat will be medium rare after this time; cook for a little longer if you prefer.

5 Meanwhile, in a bowl beat together the reserved tapenade and sour cream. Cover and set aside until required.

6 Serve the beef en croûte on a warmed serving platter garnished with rosemary sprigs. Hand the tapenade cream around separately. **Serves 6**

CITRUS BEEF WITH KUMQUATS

A rich casserole with a hint of orange – ideal for cold winter days. Serve with a large dish of creamed potatoes or small jacket potatoes. A simple mixed leafy salad is the only extra accompaniment required.

1kg (2lb) stewing steak · salt and pepper to taste
60g (2oz/½ cup) plain flour · 3 tablespoons grapeseed oil · pared rind and juice of 1 orange
1 clove garlic, crushed · 315ml (10 fl oz/1¼ cups) beef stock · 155ml (5 fl oz/⅔ cup) red wine · 1 bay leaf · 375g (12oz) celery, thickly sliced
375g (12oz) leeks, thickly sliced
125g (4oz) kumquats

To Garnish:
salad leaves

1 Preheat the oven to 160C (325F/Gas 3). Cut the beef into 2.5cm (1 inch) cubes and toss in the seasoned flour to coat evenly; shake off any excess flour. Heat the oil in a large flameproof casserole and quickly brown the beef, a few pieces at a time, on all sides.

2 Return all the beef to the pan. Add the pared orange rind, 3 tablespoons orange juice, garlic, stock, wine, bay leaf and seasoning. Bring to a simmer, cover and cook in the oven for 1 hour.

3 Add the celery, leeks and kumquats, cover and return to the oven for a further 1½ hours or until the beef is very tender. Adjust the seasoning. Serve garnished with salad leaves. **Serves 6**

BEEF & MIXED MUSHROOM POT

I usually try to buy the smoked streaky bacon in one piece from my local butcher, and cut it into thick strips. This is a good dish to prepare ahead and have ready in the freezer. Rice flavoured with toasted nuts and herbs is an ideal accompaniment.

1kg (2lb) stewing beef, cubed · salt and pepper to taste · 60g (2oz/½ cup) plain flour · 4 tablespoons grapeseed oil · 250g (8oz) button onions, peeled 185g (6oz) smoked streaky bacon, rinds removed, thinly sliced · 625ml (1 pint/2½ cups) beef stock 500g (1lb) mixed mushrooms eg. brown cap, chanterelles, ceps, parasols, oyster mushrooms

Marinade:
1 small onion, sliced · 1 small carrot, sliced · 1 stick celery, sliced · 1 clove garlic, crushed 470ml (15 fl oz/2 cups) red wine · 6 juniper berries, crushed · 2 tablespoons olive oil · few thyme sprigs

To Garnish:
thyme sprigs · parsley sprigs

1 First place all the marinade ingredients in a non-metallic bowl. Cut the beef into 4cm (1½ inch) cubes and add to the marinade. Stir well, cover and leave to marinate in the refrigerator overnight.

2 Preheat the oven to 160C (325F/Gas 3). Remove the beef from the marinade with a slotted spoon; drain. Toss the beef in the seasoned flour to coat evenly, shaking off excess flour. Strain the marinade and reserve. Heat the oil in a large flameproof casserole and quickly brown the beef, a few pieces at a time, on all sides.

3 Return all the beef to the pan. Add the strained marinade and all the remaining ingredients, except the mushrooms. Bring to the boil, cover and cook in the oven for 2 hours.

4 Add the mushrooms, cover and return to the oven for a further 30 minutes or until the beef is very tender. Adjust the seasoning. Serve garnished with thyme and parsley sprigs.

Serves 6

VEGETARIAN DISHES

From stir-fries and savoury flans to tempting bakes, tasty stuffed vegetables and colourful stews, there are mouth-watering recipes here to tempt even the most hardened carnivore! Turn to the following chapter on vegetable side dishes for suggestions to accompany these imaginative vegetarian meals.

GNOCCHI WITH WALNUT PESTO

These little dumplings are light and airy if handled carefully – a perfect foil for the rich nutty walnut sauce.

250g (8oz) ricotta or curd cheese · 60g (2oz) butter, softened · 125g (4oz) Parmesan cheese, freshly grated · 1 egg, size 2, beaten · 3 tablespoons (9tsp) plain flour · salt and pepper to taste · grated nutmeg to taste

Walnut Pesto:
1 clove garlic, crushed · 60g (2oz/⅔ cup) walnut halves · 45g (1½ oz) basil leaves, stalks removed
3 tablespoons freshly grated Parmesan cheese
155ml (5 fl oz/⅔ cup) olive oil

To Serve:
basil leaves to garnish
thinly pared Parmesan cheese

1 Sieve the ricotta or curd cheese into a bowl and add the butter, Parmesan, egg and flour. Beat until smooth, seasoning with salt, pepper and nutmeg. Cover and chill in the refrigerator for at least 1 hour or overnight.

2 Meanwhile, make the walnut pesto. Place the garlic, walnuts, basil leaves, cheese and salt in a blender or food processor and blend until smooth. With the machine still running, gradually pour in the olive oil; the pesto will thicken as the oil is absorbed.

3 Bring a large pan of salted water to the boil. Lower the heat and add heaped teaspoonfuls of gnocchi mixture to the simmering water. Poach gently for 3-4 minutes or until they rise to the surface. Remove with a slotted spoon and drain.

4 Pile the gnocchi on to warmed individual plates and top each serving with a generous dollop of pesto. Garnish with basil and serve immediately, with extra Parmesan handed separately. **Serves 3**

SPAGHETTINI WITH TOMATO SAUCE

The softer and redder the tomatoes are for this raw sauce, the better. Large beefsteak or marmande tomatoes are ideal, as are fresh ripe Italian plum tomatoes. The heat from the pasta releases the flavours of the raw tomatoes and sauce ingredients – to delicious effect.

250-300g (8-10oz) dried spaghettini or thin spaghetti

Tomato Sauce:

4 large ripe tomatoes · 4 tablespoons shredded herbs, eg. basil, majoram, oregano, parsley, or a mixture of these · 2 cloves garlic, finely chopped 125g (4oz/¾ cup) chopped black olives (optional) 125ml (4 fl oz/½ cup) olive oil · salt and pepper to taste

To Garnish:

basil or parsley sprigs

1 To make the tomato sauce, plunge the tomatoes into a pan of boiling water and leave for 1 minute. Refresh under cold water and slip off the skins. Cut the tomatoes in half, squeeze out the seeds and chop the flesh into 1cm (½ inch) cubes. Place in a bowl with the herbs, garlic and olives if using. Add all but 2 tablespoons olive oil. Season and toss gently to mix. Allow the flavours to mingle for at least 30 minutes.

2 Drop the pasta into a large pan of boiling salted water, with the remaining oil added. Cook for 5-7 minutes, according to manufacturer's instructions, until *al dente* (cooked but firm to the bite).

3 Drain thoroughly and divide between warmed serving plates. Top with the tomato sauce and garnish with basil or parsley. Serve immediately. **Serves 2-3**

FALAFEL WITH MINT DRESSING

I first tasted falafel on my first trip to the States – it seemed so American to me – straight out of the movies! Made from chick peas, this Jewish speciality is eaten as a snack or with a salad as a light meal.

250g (8oz/1 ¼ cups) chick peas, soaked overnight
1 tablespoon olive oil · 1 small egg, beaten
2 cloves garlic, crushed · pinch of chilli powder
½ teaspoon ground cumin · ½ teaspoon ground coriander · salt and pepper to taste · 8 water biscuits, crushed · olive oil for frying

Sesame Mint Dressing:
2 tablespoons tahini (sesame seed paste)
2 tablespoons olive oil · juice of ½ lemon
3 tablespoons chopped mint

To Garnish:
mint sprigs · lemon wedges

1 Drain the chick peas and pat dry with absorbent kitchen paper. Place in a blender or food processor and process until finely ground. Add the oil, egg, garlic, spices and seasoning and work until smooth. Add half of the crushed water biscuits and blend to a smooth firm paste. If the mixture is too soft to roll into balls at this stage, add more crushed water biscuit until firm enough to handle.
2 For the sesame mint dressing, whisk all the ingredients together in a bowl, adding enough water to give a pouring consistency.
3 Divide the falafel mixture into about 18-20 equal pieces, roll into balls and flatten slightly. Heat a little olive oil in a frying pan and fry the falafel in batches until golden brown, about 3 minutes on each side; drain on absorbent kitchen paper and keep warm while cooking the remainder.
4 Serve the falafel as soon as they are all cooked, garnished with mint and lemon wedges, and accompanied by the sesame mint dressing. **Serves 3-4**

VEGETABLE & NOODLE STIR-FRY

Use a potato peeler to pare long strips of carrot and courgette (zucchini) which are quickly cooked by stir-frying. Prawns or softly scrambled egg may be added at the final stage if you so wish.

220g (7oz) Chinese egg noodles · 2 teaspoons sesame oil · 3 tablespoons groundnut or sunflower oil · 1 clove garlic, crushed · 1-2 red chillies, sliced 3 small carrots, pared into strips · 3 small courgettes (zucchini), pared into strips · 4 spring onions (green shallots), sliced · 125g (4oz) small cup mushrooms · 125g (4oz) mange tout (snow peas), topped and tailed · 2 teaspoons cornflour 125ml (4 fl oz/½ cup) vegetable stock or water 3 tablespoons soy sauce · large pinch of sugar 125g (4oz) short sprouted beans · 1 tablespoon snipped chives · 1 tablespoon chopped coriander · salt and pepper

1 Cook the noodles in boiling water according to packet instructions. Drain and toss in the sesame oil. Set aside.

2 Heat the groundnut or sunflower oil in a wok or large frying pan. Add the garlic, chillies, carrot and courgette (zucchini) strips and stir-fry for 2 minutes. Stir in the spring onions (shallots), mushrooms and mange tout (snow peas) and continue stir-frying for 1 minute.

3 Blend the cornflour with a little of the stock or water. Add the rest of the stock or water to the wok with the soy sauce and sugar and simmer for 2 minutes. Add the cornflour mixture and cook, stirring, until thickened. Stir in the sprouted beans, chives and coriander and season with salt and pepper to taste.

4 Add the noodles to the wok and stir-fry for 1-2 minutes until heated through. Transfer to a warmed serving dish and serve immediately. **Serves 3-4**

VARIATION: Omit the chillies. Add 2.5cm (1 inch) piece fresh root (green) ginger, finely chopped, and 1 red or yellow pepper, seeded and sliced, with the garlic.

GRILLED VEGETABLES WITH NUT PASTE

Simply grilled vegetables are delicious served with garlicky toasted walnut paste and crusty bread. You can make the walnut paste a day or two ahead and keep it covered in the refrigerator. You could also include other vegetables such as aubergine (eggplant), corn cobs and tomatoes.

1 red pepper · 1 yellow pepper · 8 large flat mushrooms · 6 small courgettes (zucchini), halved 1 tablespoon lemon juice · 2 tablespoons olive oil salt and pepper to taste

Nut Paste:

90g (3oz) walnut pieces · 1 clove garlic, crushed 1 tablespoon chopped parsley · 60ml (2 fl oz/¼ cup) walnut oil · 60ml (2 fl oz/¼ cup) groundnut or sunflower oil · 1-2 teaspoons lemon juice

1 First prepare the toasted walnut paste. Preheat the grill. Spread the walnuts on a baking sheet and toast for 3-4 minutes, shaking to turn, until dark golden. Place the walnuts, garlic and parsley in a blender or food processor. Process for a few seconds to chop finely, then, with the motor running, slowly pour in the oils to give a paste. Add lemon juice to taste and seasoning. Set aside.

2 Halve and seed the peppers, then cut each half lengthwise into 3 wide strips. Arrange on a baking sheet, skin side up, with the mushrooms and courgettes (zucchini).

3 Mix together the lemon juice and olive oil and use to brush the mushrooms and courgettes (zucchini). Sprinkle the vegetables lightly with salt and pepper. Cook under the preheated grill for 5-10 minutes, rearranging as necessary, until the peppers are browned and blistered and the courgettes (zucchini) and mushrooms are just tender. Transfer the vegetables to a plate as they are cooked and keep warm.

4 Serve the grilled vegetables with toasted walnut paste and chunks of crusty bread. **Serves 3-4**

VEGETABLE KEBABS

Few vegetarian recipes can be cooked on a barbecue – here's one that is suitable. A rosemary brush is ideal for basting kebabs on a barbecue and imparts a delicate flavour – tie a few sprigs of rosemary together, twining string around the stalks to make the handle.

375g (12oz) aubergines (eggplants), preferably small pink ones · salt and pepper to taste · 500g (1lb) baby new potatoes · 1 red pepper · 4 small onions · 125ml (4 fl oz/½ cup) olive oil · 1 clove garlic, finely chopped · 125g (4oz) button mushrooms · 8 bay leaves

Watercress Dressing:
1 bunch watercress, chopped · 1 clove garlic
1 teaspoon clear honey · 1 tablespoon lemon juice
2 spring onions (green shallots), chopped
90ml (3 fl oz/⅓ cup) natural yogurt
90ml (3 fl oz/⅓ cup) thick mayonnaise

1 Cut the aubergines (eggplants) into 2.5cm (1 inch) pieces and put into a colander. Sprinkle with salt and leave to drain for 30 minutes. Rinse and pat dry with absorbent kitchen paper.

2 Cook the potatoes in boiling salted water for 10 minutes until tender; drain. Halve and seed the red pepper, then cut into squares. Cut the onions into quarters.

3 Put the oil and garlic into a bowl, add the aubergine (eggplant) and mushrooms and turn until evenly coated.

4 Thread the aubergine (eggplant), onions, mushrooms, pepper, potatoes and bay leaves alternately on to 8 large skewers. Brush thoroughly with the remaining oil and garlic.

5 To make the watercress dressing, put all the ingredients except the mayonnaise in a blender or food processor and work to a purée. Fold into the mayonnaise until smooth.

6 Grill or barbecue the kebabs for 10-15 minutes, turning occasionally and basting frequently with oil. Serve with the watercress dressing. **Serves 4**

FRITTERS WITH WALNUT SAUCE

The dipping sauce for these light vegetables fritters is a more gutsy version of pesto. The vegetables I have used are suggestions only.

Walnut Sauce:
2 cloves garlic, crushed · 12 basil sprigs
4 walnut halves · 5 tablespoons olive oil · salt and pepper to taste

Fritters:
125g (4oz/1 cup) self-raising flour · 1 teaspoon salt
250ml (8fl oz/1 cup) water · ½ cauliflower
250g (8oz) courgettes (zucchini) · 1 red pepper
oil for deep frying

To Garnish:
basil sprigs

1 To make the walnut sauce, grind the garlic, basil and walnuts using a pestle and mortar or clean coffee grinder until smooth. Gradually work in the olive oil to form a thick sauce. Season with salt and pepper.

2 To make the fritters, sift the flour and salt into a bowl. Gradually add the water, beating all the time, to form a smooth batter. Cut the cauliflower into florets, the courgettes (zucchini) into thick slices and the red pepper into broad strips. Add to the batter and stir carefully until all the vegetables are well coated.

3 Heat the oil to 180C (350F), or until a little batter added to the pan rises to the surface instantly, surrounded by bubbles. Fry the vegetables in batches in the hot oil for 2-3 minutes, until the batter is golden brown and crisp. Drain on absorbent kitchen paper and keep warm while frying the remaining vegetables.

4 Serve the vegetables on a warm serving platter with the bowl of walnut sauce, or on individual plates with a spoonful of sauce. Garnish with basil. **Serves 3**

VARIATION: Try using other vegetables for the fritters, such as whole button mushrooms, fennel slices or carrot sticks.

STIR-FRY WITH GREMOLATA

Gremolata is a combination of chopped parsley, garlic and lemon. Usually it is sprinkled over veal dishes, but I find it's delicious sprinkled over a selection of crunchy vegetables.

250g (8oz) broccoli · 250g (8oz) cauliflower 2 medium-sized leeks · 125g (4oz) mange tout (snow peas) · 2 carrots, peeled · 2 tablespoons sunflower oil · salt and pepper to taste

Gremolata:

1 teaspoon grated lemon rind · 1 clove garlic, finely chopped · 3 tablespoons chopped parsley

1 Cut the broccoli and cauliflower into small florets. Thinly slice the leeks. Top and tail the mange tout (snow peas). Using a potato peeler, pare the carrots into thin ribbons.

2 To make the gremolata, place the lemon rind, garlic and parsley in a small bowl and mix well.

3 Heat the oil in a frying pan with a lid, or a wok. Add the leeks, broccoli and cauliflower and stir-fry for 1 minute until the leeks start to soften. Add the carrot strips and stir-fry for a futher 1 minute.

4 Add 2 tablespoons water, cover and cook for 4 minutes, until the vegetables are just tender. Add the mange tout (snow peas), salt and pepper. Stir well, cover and cook for 1 minute.

5 Turn into a warmed serving dish and sprinkle with the gremolata. Serve immediately, with crusty bread as a light meal, or with other dishes. **Serves 4**

VARIATION: Replace the carrots with courgette ribbons and use 1 large red pepper, seeded and sliced, in place of the mange tout.

SWEET PEPPER & BASIL TRANCHE

Loose-based oblong fluted tranche tins are excellent for all kinds of flans – sweet and savoury. They cook evenly and the flans are easy to cut and serve. If you haven't one or can't find one to buy, use a 20cm (8 inch) round flan tin instead. Serve this tasty flan with cherry tomato and bean salad (page 74) and a crisp leafy salad, plus plenty of warm French bread.

410g (13oz) packet shortcrust pastry · 2 large red peppers, about 375g (12oz) total weight
155g (5oz) full-fat soft cheese with garlic and herbs
2 eggs · large pinch of powdered saffron
2 tablespoons chopped parsley · 1 tablespoon chopped basil · salt and pepper to taste

To Garnish:
herb sprigs

1 Preheat the oven to 200C (400F/Gas 6). Roll out the pastry on a lightly floured surface and use to line a 30 × 11cm (12 × 4½ inch) tranche tin. Chill for 15 minutes. Line with greaseproof paper and baking beans and bake blind for about 15 minutes or until the pastry edges are pale golden. Remove the paper and beans and bake for a further 5 minutes to cook the base. Lower oven temperature to 180C (350F/Gas 4).

2 Preheat grill to high and grill the peppers for 10-12 minutes, turning frequently, until the skin is charred. Cool slightly, then rub off the skins under cold running water. Pat dry with absorbent kitchen paper. Halve the peppers, remove the core and seeds, then roughly chop the flesh.

3 In a bowl, whisk together the soft cheese, eggs, saffron and chopped herbs until smooth. Stir in the peppers and seasoning.

4 Spoon the filling into the prepared flan case and bake in the oven for 25 minutes or until just set. Serve garnished with herbs.

Serves 6

NOTE: If you prefer to make your own shortcrust pastry, use a 185g (6oz/1¼ cup) flour quantity.

STUFFED AUBERGINES (EGGPLANTS)

These are excellent on their own, or with a salad. You can prepare them in advance and bake just before serving.

4 small aubergines (eggplants), halved lengthwise
4 tablespoons virgin olive oil

Tomato Sauce:
500ml (16 fl oz/2 cups) passata · 1 clove garlic, crushed · 1 bay leaf

Filling:
60g (2oz) butter · 1 onion, finely chopped · 1 clove garlic, crushed · 375g (12oz) button mushrooms, chopped · 30g (1oz) dried ceps (porcini), soaked in warm water for 20 minutes and chopped
2 tablespoons finely chopped coriander · salt and pepper to taste · 2 tablespoons dried breadcrumbs
1 tablespoon sesame seeds (optional)

To Garnish:
coriander sprigs

1 First make the tomato sauce. Put all the ingredients in a saucepan, bring to the boil and cook until thickened and reduced by half. Discard the bay leaf. Set aside.

2 Meanwhile, preheat the oven to 180C (350F/Gas 4). Scoop out the flesh from the aubergines (eggplants) with a spoon, leaving 1cm (½ inch) thick shells. Finely chop the flesh. Arrange the shells in an oiled baking dish, brush the insides liberally with oil and bake in the preheated oven for 10 minutes.

3 To make the filling, heat the butter in a large frying pan. Add the onion and garlic and sauté for 3 minutes to soften. Add the chopped aubergine (eggplant) flesh, mushrooms and ceps (porcini); cook for 4-5 minutes until just tender. Stir in the coriander and seasoning.

4 Divide the tomato sauce between the aubergine (eggplant) shells. Cover with the mushroom mixture and sprinkle with breadcrumbs and sesame seeds, if using. Return to the oven and bake for 15 minutes. Serve hot, garnished with coriander. **Serves 4**

CARROT & CELERIAC BAKE

This purée of carrot and celeriac enriched with eggs and grated cheese is substantial enough to serve as a warming winter meal.
Serve it with baked tomatoes, a green vegetable and crusty bread.

500g (1 lb) carrots · 500g (1 lb) celeriac · 30g (1 oz) butter · salt and pepper to taste · 2 teaspoons chopped thyme (optional) · freshly grated nutmeg 3 eggs, beaten · 90g (3oz) gruyère cheese, grated 1 tablespoon fresh breadcrumbs

To Garnish:
parsley or thyme sprigs

1 Peel the carrots and celeriac and cut them into even-sized chunks. Cook in boiling salted water for 15-20 minutes, until tender.

2 Preheat the oven to 180C (350F/Gas 4). Drain and mash the vegetables together, or purée them in a blender or food processor. Add the butter, salt, pepper, thyme if using, and nutmeg; mix well. Stir in the beaten eggs and 60g (2oz/½ cup) of the cheese.

3 Turn the mixture into a buttered ovenproof dish and sprinkle with the breadcrumbs and remaining cheese. Bake in the oven for 35-40 minutes, until risen and golden brown. Serve hot, garnished with parsley or thyme sprigs.

Serves 4

VARIATION: Use either swede or turnip in place of the celeriac. Flavour the bake with chopped parsley rather than thyme.

COURGETTE (ZUCCHINI) BAKE

This is an ideal choice when you are looking for a dish that can be completely assembled well in advance. Make it in the summer when the tomatoes are full of flavour. Serve with crusty bread as a light lunch or supper.

750g (1 ½ lb) courgettes (zucchini) · 500g (1 lb) ripe tomatoes · 4 tablespoons olive oil · 2 onions, thinly sliced · 2 teaspoons chopped thyme salt and pepper to taste · 1 tablespoon grated Parmesan cheese

1 Preheat the oven to 190C (375F/Gas 5). Top and tail the courgettes (zucchini), then cut into thin diagonal slices. Skin the tomatoes and cut into thin slices. Heat half the oil in a frying pan, add the onions and fry for 5-8 minutes, until they are soft and lightly browned.

2 Spread the onions over the base of a greased shallow ovenproof dish. Arrange alternate layers of courgettes (zucchini) and tomatoes over the onions, making sure each layer overlaps the previous one. Drizzle with the remaining oil and sprinkle with thyme, salt and pepper.

3 Bake in the preheated oven for 35-45 minutes. Sprinkle with the Parmesan and bake for a further 10 minutes. Serve hot.

Serves 4

NOTE: To skin tomatoes, spear on a fork and hold over a gas flame for 15-30 seconds, turning until the skin blisters, then peel away the skins. Alternatively plunge into a bowl of boiling hot water and leave for 30 seconds, then peel.

VARIATION: For a more substantial supper dish, add 1 aubergine (eggplant) and 1 red pepper to the base; chop and fry with the onions.

CORIANDER-SPICED VEGETABLES

Serve this lightly spiced curry with naan or pita bread, or with rice and other curry dishes.

2 onions · 3 cloves garlic · 2 red or green chilies
1-inch piece ginger root · 2 lb. mixed vegetables, such as potatoes, cauliflower, green beans, carrots
1 tablespoon coriander seeds · 2 teaspoons cumin seeds · 1 bay leaf · 2 tablespoons oil
1 ¼ cups canned chopped tomatoes · 1 cup water
salt and pepper to taste · ½ cup frozen peas
2 tablespoons chopped cilantro leaves

To Garnish:
cilantro sprigs

1 Slice the onions thinly. Finely chop the garlic. Halve, seed and finely chop the chilies. Peel and finely chop the ginger. Peel the potatoes. Trim the rest of the vegetables and cut into even-sized chunks.

2 Crush the coriander and cumin seeds in a clean coffee grinder, or using a mortar and pestle. Break the bay leaf into several pieces.

3 Heat the oil in a large saucepan. Add the onion and fry for about 5 minutes, until softened and lightly colored. Add the garlic, chilies, ginger and bay leaf and fry for 2 to 3 minutes, stirring all the time. Add the ground spices and mix well. Add all the vegetables, except the cauliflower and peas, stirring them around to coat with the spices.

4 Add the tomatoes, water, salt and pepper. Bring to a boil, cover and simmer for 10 minutes, then add the cauliflower, peas and cilantro leaves. Cook for 15-20 minutes longer until the vegetables are tender. Serve garnished with cilantro sprigs. **Serves 4 to 6**

SPINACH STUFFED POTATOES

I use medium-sized potatoes for this recipe as they cook more quickly than large ones and look attractive. When spinach is out of season you can substitute 125g (4oz) frozen spinach.

6 potatoes, about 185g (6oz) each · 250g (8oz) spinach · 30g (1oz) butter · 2 shallots, peeled and chopped · ¼ teaspoon allspice · salt and pepper to taste · 2 tablespoons grated Parmesan cheese

1 Preheat the oven to 200C (400F/Gas 6). Scrub the potatoes and pat dry with kitchen paper. Bake in the oven for about 45 minutes, until tender. When cool enough to handle, cut the potatoes in half and scoop out the flesh into a bowl. Mash thoroughly.

2 Wash the spinach in several changes of water; drain well. Melt the butter in a saucepan, add the shallots and cook for about 5 minutes until softened. Add the spinach and cook until just wilted, then cover and cook for 5 minutes, until tender. Add the potato, allspice, salt and pepper and mix well.

3 Place the potato shells in an ovenproof dish. Fill with the spinach mixture and sprinkle with cheese. Return to the oven for 20 minutes, until the topping is golden brown. Serve hot as a snack, or accompanied by a mixed salad as a light meal. **Serves 4-6**

VARIATION: Replace the spinach with 3-4 tomatoes, skinned and finely chopped. Flavour the potato filling with 1 tablespoon finely chopped basil instead of allspice.

STUFFED VEGETABLES

These stuffed vegetables are equally good served warm or cold. They also reheat well.

125ml (4 fl oz/½ cup) virgin olive oil · 4 spring onions (green shallots), chopped · 185g (6oz/ 1¼ cups) long grain rice · 125g (4oz/1 cup) dried apricots, chopped · small bunch of parsley, chopped ¼ teaspoon ground allspice · ¼ teaspoon cayenne pepper · salt and pepper to taste · 250ml (8 fl oz/ 1 cup) water · 4 tomatoes · 2 red or green peppers 2 small aubergines (eggplants) · 2 courgettes (zucchini) · 2 tablespoons tomato purée (paste)

1 Preheat the oven to 180C (350F/Gas 4). Heat the oil in a saucepan, add the spring onions (shallots) and fry for 1 minute. Add the rice and stir well to coat. Add the apricots, parsley, allspice, cayenne, salt, pepper and water. Bring to the boil, then lower the heat, partially cover and cook for 10 minutes, until the rice is almost tender.

2 Remove the tops from the tomatoes and scoop out the seeds. Halve and seed the peppers. Halve the aubergines (eggplants) and courgettes (zucchini) lengthwise and scoop out some of the flesh. (Use the scooped out flesh for another dish.)

3 Place the vegetables in a buttered ovenproof dish or roasting tin and carefully fill them with the rice stuffing. Dilute the tomato purée (paste) with 500ml (16fl oz/ 2 cups) hot water and pour over the vegetables. Bake, uncovered, in the preheated oven for 45-55 minutes, until the vegetables are tender. **Serves 4**

SUMMER VEGETABLE STEW

Use the sweetest, smallest early vegetables for this delightfully colourful dish. Serve it with crusty bread to mop up the juices.

juice of 1 lemon · 4 baby artichokes · 2 ripe tomatoes · 4 shallots · 125g (4oz) baby carrots 500g (1lb) broad beans in pods · 125g (4oz) French beans · 250g (8oz) small new potatoes 2 tablespoons olive oil · 125ml (4 fl oz/½ cup) dry white wine · 125ml (4 fl oz/½ cup) vegetable stock or water · 1 bouquet garni · salt and pepper to taste

1 Add the lemon juice to a bowl of water large enough to hold the artichokes. Trim the tops off the artichokes and remove any tough outside leaves. Cut the artichokes down through the heart into quarters and remove the chokes if they have formed. Place the artichokes in the lemon water with a saucer on top to keep them submerged.

2 Skin, seed and chop the tomatoes. Peel the shallots and cut each one into quarters, almost to the base. Scrape and trim the carrots, pod the broad beans, trim the French beans and scrub the potatoes.

3 Heat the oil in a saucepan, add the shallots and fry for 2-3 minutes, until lightly browned. Drain the artichokes and add to the pan, stirring well to coat in the oil. Add the wine, stock or water, bouquet garni, salt and pepper. Bring to the boil, cover the pan and simmer for 15 minutes.

4 Add the tomatoes, carrots, broad beans, French beans and potatoes. Bring back to the boil, lower the heat and cook for a further 25-30 minutes, until all the vegetables are tender. Remove the bouquet garni before serving.

Serves 4-6

VEGETABLE SIDE DISHES

Serving tasty vegetable accompaniments adds interest and variety to meals. Sample artichoke hearts with pistachios; glazed baby turnips; or tender young spinach with pine nuts; for example. With these recipes you will be able to make the most of vegetables in season – when they are always at their best.

BROCCOLI & ORANGE BUTTER SAUCE

This is particularly good with cape broccoli and romanesco cauliflower – as they both have a tender melting texture. Serve as an accompaniment to grilled meat or poultry.

500g (1lb) broccoli

Orange Butter Sauce:
4 tablespoons fresh orange juice · 1 tablespoon tarragon vinegar · salt and pepper to taste 125g (4oz) unsalted butter · 2-3 tablespoons hot vegetable stock

To Garnish:
orange rind shreds

1 Cut the broccoli into florets and steam or cook in boiling salted water until just tender, about 7-10 minutes; drain.
2 Meanwhile make the sauce. Place the orange juice, vinegar, salt and pepper in a small pan. Bring to the boil and boil rapidly until reduced to 1 tablespoon.
3 Remove from the heat and whisk in the butter, a piece at a time, until a smooth creamy sauce is formed. If the sauce becomes too thick, whisk very briefly over the heat.
4 Gradually whisk in enough stock to yield a pouring consistency. Pour the sauce over the broccoli and garnish with orange shreds. **Serves 4**

MUSTARD & CORIANDER CAULIFLOWER

Fresh coriander and mustard seeds add a delicious flavour to cauliflower. Serve with curries and other spicy dishes.

1 cauliflower · 2 tablespoons oil
2 teaspoons black mustard seeds
2 tablespoons chopped coriander leaves
4 tablespoons water · salt and pepper to taste

To Garnish:
coriander sprigs

1 Cut the cauliflower into florets. Heat the oil in a wok or frying pan with a lid, add the mustard seeds and fry until they start to pop. Add the cauliflower and stir until evenly coated with mustard seeds. Cook, stirring for about 10 minutes.

2 Add the remaining ingredients and stir well. Cover and cook for 10-15 minutes, until the cauliflower is tender, but retains some crunch. Serve hot, garnished with coriander sprigs. **Serves 4-6**

GRILLED MUSTARD TOMATOES

Use large ripe tomatoes which have a full sweet flavour to offset the sharp mustard in this piquant dressing.

4-6 large tomatoes

Dressing:
1 tablespoon olive oil · 1 tablespoon lemon juice 1 teaspoon clear honey · 1 teaspoon wholegrain mustard · salt to taste

To Garnish:
chopped parsley

1 Preheat the grill to medium. Cut the tomatoes in half and place on the grill rack.

2 Mix together the dressing ingredients in a small bowl and brush over the tomatoes. Grill for about 5 minutes, basting occasionally. Sprinkle with chopped parsley and serve hot.

Serves 4

ARTICHOKE HEARTS & PISTACHIOS

Serve this pretty vegetable dish either as an elegant accompaniment or starter.

juice of 2 lemons · 4 large artichokes · salt and pepper to taste · 30g (1oz) shelled pistachio nuts 60g (2oz) butter · 1 tablespoon chopped parsley

1 Add the lemon juice to a bowl of water large enough to hold the artichoke hearts. Using a sharp knife, remove the top half of an artichoke. Strip off the tough outer leaves, then cut the artichoke into quarters. Working quickly, remove the hairy choke in each quarter and trim off any tough leaves. Place in the water with a saucer on top to keep it submerged. Prepare the other artichokes in the same way.

2 Transfer the artichokes and lemon water to a large saucepan and add salt. Bring to the boil, cover and simmer for 15-20 minutes, until the artichokes are tender; drain.

3 Meanwhile, place the pistachios in a small bowl and cover with boiling water. Leave for 5 minutes, then drain and slip off the skins. Chop the pistachios.

4 Melt the butter in a saucepan, add the artichokes and fry for 2-3 minutes. Add the nuts, pepper and parsley. Heat through and serve immediately. **Serves 4**

SWEET & SOUR MUSHROOMS

Serve these mushrooms in their rich sauce as an accompaniment to grills, kebabs or barbecued foods. Alternatively, serve them as a starter with crusty bread.

2 tablespoons sunflower oil · 1 small onion, chopped
1 stick celery, chopped · 500g (1 lb) cup mushrooms, sliced · 1 tablespoon Worcestershire sauce
125ml (4 fl oz/1/2 cup) red wine · 2 teaspoons French mustard · 2 tablespoons soft brown sugar
salt and pepper to taste

To Garnish:
shredded spring onion (green shallot)

1 Heat the oil in a saucepan, add the onion and celery and fry until softened, about 5 minutes.
2 Add the mushrooms and stir well. Add the remaining ingredients and bring to the boil, stirring all the time. Simmer, uncovered, for 15-20 minutes, until the mushrooms are tender and the sauce is slightly thickened.
3 Serve hot, garnished with spring onion (shallot), as a starter or accompaniment. **Serves 4-6**

BROAD BEANS WITH PEPPERCORNS

Fresh broad beans are an early summer treat, when they are cooked young and sweet. Avoid pods where the beans are almost bursting out as the flavour won't be nearly as good. Serve this side dish with succulent spring lamb.

1.5kg (3lb) broad beans · few marjoram sprigs few thyme sprigs · 1 teaspoon green peppercorns 30g (1 oz) butter · 2 teaspoons plain flour 125ml (4 fl oz/½ cup) dry white wine · salt and pepper to taste

1 Pod the broad beans and place in a pan with the herbs and enough water to just cover. Bring to the boil, then lower the heat, cover and cook for about 10 minutes until just tender. Drain, reserving the cooking liquor.

2 Meanwhile coarsely crush the peppercorns and mix into the butter. Melt the butter in a saucepan, add the flour and cook for 1 minute. Stir in the wine and cook, stirring, until thickened and smooth. Add 4-5 tablespoons of the reserved liquor, stirring until the sauce just coats the back of the spoon. Season well.

3 Add the broad beans to the sauce and heat through gently before serving. **Serves 6-8**

BRAISED AUBERGINES (EGGPLANTS)

Serve these tasty aubergines (eggplants) hot or cold as an accompaniment, salad or starter.

500g (1 lb) aubergines (eggplants) · salt and pepper to taste · 3 tablespoons olive oil · 1 clove garlic, crushed · 1 teaspoon chopped oregano or ½ teaspoon dried · 1 teaspoon paprika

1 Cut the aubergines (eggplants) into 2.5cm (1 inch) chunks and place in a colander. Sprinkle with salt and leave to drain for 30 minutes. Rinse and pat dry with kitchen paper.

2 Heat the oil in a saucepan, add the aubergines (eggplants) and fry for about 5 minutes, stirring all the time. Add the garlic and cook for 1 minute. Stir in the oregano, paprika, salt and pepper. Lower the heat, cover and cook for 15-20 minutes, until the aubergines (eggplants) are tender but not mushy. Serve hot or allow to cool before serving. **Serves 4**

GRATIN DAUPHINOIS

This is a useful accompaniment to prepare in advance, especially if you are entertaining. Serve it with roasts, grilled meats or barbecued foods.

30g (1 oz) butter · 750g (1 ½lb) potatoes · salt and pepper · 2 cloves garlic, finely chopped
315ml (10 fl oz/1 ¼ cups) double (thick) cream

1 Preheat the oven to 190C (375F/Gas 5). Grease a shallow ovenproof dish liberally with half of the butter.
2 Slice the potatoes thinly and arrange in the dish, sprinkling salt, pepper and garlic between each layer.
3 Pour over the cream to three-quarters fill the dish and dot with the remaining butter. Bake in the oven for about 1 ½ hours, until golden brown on top. **Serves 6**

GLAZED BABY TURNIPS

Use small sweet turnips and only peel them if the skins are tough. These are delicious served with duck or pork.

500g (1 lb) baby turnips · 2 teaspoons sugar
60g (2oz) butter · salt and pepper to taste
125ml (4 fl oz/½ cup) water

1 Trim the turnips, leaving a little tuft of stalk on each. Peel or scrub them, then place in a small saucepan with the sugar, butter, salt, pepper and water. Bring to the boil, then cover and cook gently for 10-12 minutes, until the turnips are just tender.

2 Remove the lid and boil hard to reduce the liquid to a glaze. Serve hot.

Serves 4

SPINACH WITH PINE NUTS

A tasty accompaniment to serve hot with kebabs, grilled meat or fish. It can also be served cold as a salad – refresh the spinach in cold running water immediately after cooking and stir in a little extra yogurt.

1kg (2lb) spinach leaves · salt and pepper to taste freshly grated nutmeg · 1 tablespoon sunflower oil 1 clove garlic, finely chopped · 2 tablespoons pine nuts · 2 tablespoons raisins · 2 tablespoons thick Greek yogurt

1 Wash the spinach in several changes of cold water, picking out any discoloured leaves. Place the spinach in a saucepan with just the water clinging to the leaves after washing. Season with salt, pepper and nutmeg to taste and heat gently until the spinach leaves start to wilt. Shake the pan, cover and cook gently for 3-5 minutes until the spinach is tender.

2 Drain the spinach in a colander, pressing out as much liquid as possible. Chop the leaves using the edge of a saucer.

3 Heat the oil in a frying pan. Add the garlic, pine nuts and raisins and fry gently for about 2 minutes until the pine nuts are pale golden. Add the spinach, stir well and heat through. Stir in the yogurt, then taste and add more seasoning if necessary. Serve immediately.

Serves 4-6

Desserts

This splendid collection of mouth-watering desserts features fresh fruit recipes; light, airy soufflés and mousses; warming puddings and pies; and refreshing iced desserts. Whatever the occasion and the season you will find a suitable dessert in this chapter.

TANGY LEMON MOUSSE

This simple, foolproof lemon mousse is absolutely delicious. Prepare it the day before serving and refrigerate overnight to allow the flavours to develop.

375ml (12 fl oz/1 ½ cups) condensed milk
315ml (10 fl oz/1 ¼ cups) whipping cream
grated rind and juice of 4 large lemons

To Decorate:
lemon slices
mint sprigs (optional)

1 Put the condensed milk and cream into a large bowl and whisk with an electric beater until the mixture becomes thick enough to leave a ribbon when the beaters are lifted.

2 With the motor still running, slowly add the lemon rind and juice; the mixture will suddenly thicken. Immediately stop whisking and transfer the mousse to individual serving dishes. Chill overnight.

3 Serve decorated with lemon slices and mint sprigs if desired. **Serves 6-8**

SUMMER FRUIT FOOL

A 'fool' is really just a mixture of fruit purée and cream. You can make it less rich by replacing some of the cream with yogurt or fromage frais.
Any seasonal fruits can be used – fresh soft fruits, such as raspberries or strawberries – or stewed gooseberries, apricots or rhubarb.
Serve fools simply in glass dishes, or more elegantly in these tuile baskets.

Tuile Baskets:
30g (1oz/¼ cup) plain flour · 60g (2oz/¼ cup) caster sugar · 1 egg white · 30g (1oz) butter, melted

Fool:
315g (10oz) summer fruits, such as strawberries, raspberries etc.
60g (2oz/¼ cup) caster sugar · 315ml (10 fl oz/ 1¼ cups) double (thick) cream

To Decorate:
strawberry or raspberry leaves

1 To make the baskets, preheat the oven to 190C (375F/Gas 5). Grease and flour 2 or 3 baking sheets. Mix the flour and sugar together in a bowl, add the egg white and melted butter, then beat thoroughly until smooth.
2 Place 7 spoonfuls of the mixture, well apart, on the baking sheets; spread thinly to 13cm (5 inch) rounds.
3 Bake one tray at a time for 6-7 minutes, until golden round the edges. Leave to cool slightly, then carefully remove each biscuit with a sharp knife and place top side down over the base of an inverted glass. Mould each biscuit to form a basket with wavy edges. Hold in position until set, then carefully remove. (As the mixture will make 7 tuiles, this allows for a breakage.)
4 To make the fool, put the fruit into a blender or food processor with the sugar and blend to a purée. Press through a nylon sieve to remove pips.
5 Whip the cream until it holds its shape firmly, then fold in the fruit purée. Spoon the fruit fool into the tuile baskets and decorate with strawberry or raspberry leaves. Serve immediately. **Serves 6**

BLACKCURRANT PARFAIT

Serve this refreshing mousse in tall glasses to show the layers. Use fresh or frozen blackcurrants.

500g (1lb) blackcurrants · 315ml (10 fl oz/ 1¼ cups) crème de cassis · 15g (½oz/5 teaspoons) powdered gelatine · 220g (7oz/⅞ cup) caster sugar 185ml (6 fl oz/¾ cup) water · 2 egg whites 315ml (10 fl oz/1¼ cups) whipping cream

To Decorate:
blackcurrants and leaves

1 If using fresh blackcurrants, wash them and remove the stalks. Place a tablespoonful of blackcurrants in each of 6 glasses. Add a tablespoonful of the crème de cassis to each serving and set aside.

2 Put 2 tablespoons crème de cassis in a small bowl, sprinkle on the gelatine and leave until spongy.

3 Put 155g (5oz/⅔ cup) of the sugar in a small pan with the water and heat gently until the sugar has dissolved. Bring to the boil and cook for 1 minute.

4 Put the rest of the blackcurrants in a blender or food processor with half of the sugar syrup and the remaining crème de cassis and work to a purée. Pass through a fine nylon sieve, then pour two thirds into a bowl. Put the other third into another bowl, with the remaining sugar syrup.

5 Warm the gelatine over a pan of hot water until it has dissolved, then stir half into each bowl of purée.

6 Chill the two-thirds portion of purée until beginning to set. Meanwhile, whisk the egg whites until stiff peaks form, then gradually whisk in the remaining sugar until thick and glossy. Whip the cream until soft peaks form. Stir a little of the cream and meringue into the chilled purée to lighten it, then fold in the remainder. Spoon the mousse into the glasses and chill until set.

7 Spoon the blackcurrant jelly over the mousses. Allow to set, then decorate with blackcurrants. **Serves 6**

ORANGE & MINT JELLY

This simple, refreshing jelly doesn't have any added sugar – making it perfect for slimmers.

15g (½oz/5 teaspoons) powdered gelatine
500g (16 fl oz/2 cups) fresh orange juice
1 tablespoon Grand Marnier · about 40 mint leaves
10 oranges

To Decorate:
mint sprigs

1 Soak the gelatine in 2 tablespoons orange juice until spongy. Bring the remaining orange juice to the boil in a pan and skim the surface. Add the gelatine and stir until dissolved. Add the grand marnier. Allow to cool.
2 Pour a 5mm (¼ inch) layer of jelly into a 940ml (1½ pint/3¾ cup) terrine. Chill until set. Wash and dry the mint leaves. Peel and segment the oranges, discarding all pith.
3 When the jelly has set, cover with a layer of mint leaves, then 2 layers of orange segments. Pour over enough jelly to cover and refrigerate until set. Add another layer of mint leaves followed by a further 2 layers of orange segments; set aside any remaining segments for decoration. Pour the remaining jelly over the top. Chill until firm.
4 To unmould, run a small knife around the sides of the jelly, then dip the terrine into hot water for a few seconds and invert the jelly on to a plate. Cut into slices, using a sharp knife. Serve, decorated with orange segments and mint. **Serves 6-8**

ORANGE SOUFFLÉS

Cooking these light, individual hot soufflés in their scooped-out orange skins makes them all the more exciting!

4 oranges · 250ml (8 fl oz/1 cup) milk · 1 vanilla pod, split · 3 egg yolks · 60g (2oz/¼ cup) caster sugar · 30g (1oz/¼ cup) plain flour · 60ml (2 fl oz/¼ cup) Grand Marnier · 4 egg whites

To Serve:

2 pink grapefruit · 3 passion fruit, halved
1-2 tablespoons honey · 1 teaspoon arrowroot, blended with 2 teaspoons cold water

1 Preheat the oven to 200C (400F/Gas 6). Halve the oranges crosswise and carefully remove the segments, as though you were preparing a grapefruit. Remove the membrane from the orange shells and discard. Place the orange halves on a baking tray and divide the orange segments between them; set aside.

2 Put the milk and vanilla pod in a saucepan and bring to the boil. In a bowl, whisk together the egg yolks and all but 1 tablespoon of the sugar until thick and light. Lightly stir in the flour. Stir in a little of the hot milk, then add to the milk in the pan. Cook, stirring, for 1 minute until thickened. Stir in the liqueur. Discard vanilla pod.

3 Whisk the egg whites until stiff peaks form. Add the remaining 1 tablespoon of sugar and whisk for 1 minute. Lightly fold into the warm crême patissière.

4 Spoon the soufflé mixture into the orange shells. Bake for 7-10 minutes until well risen and golden.

5 Meanwhile, squeeze the juice from 1 grapefruit and place in a small pan with the passion fruit pulp and honey. Warm the sauce and skim the surface. Add the blended arrowroot and cook, stirring, until slightly thickened. Sieve to remove the passion fruit seeds if preferred. Peel and segment the other grapefruit.

6 Serve the hot soufflés immediately, on individual plates, surrounded by the sauce and decorated with grapefruit segments.

Serves 4-8

SOUFFLÉS MONTE CRISTO

These irresistible chilled coffee soufflés conceal a fresh apricot and ratafia filling. Serve them accompanied by extra ratafia biscuits.
To prepare the paper collars, cut 6 pieces of non-stick paper large enough to wrap around the ramekins and stand 4cm (1½ inches) above the rims. Secure these in position with string.

125g (4oz) coffee beans · 500ml (16 fl oz/2 cups) milk · 15g (½oz/5 teaspoons) powdered gelatine 6 tablespoons tia maria or other coffee liqueur 6 egg yolks · 75g (2½oz/5 tablespoons) caster sugar · 375ml (12 fl oz/1½ cups) double (thick) cream · 2 egg whites · 250g (8oz) ripe apricots 125g (4oz) ratafias

To Decorate:
whipped cream · apricot slices

1 Secure paper collars around 6 ramekins. Coarsely grind the coffee beans and place in a heavy-based pan with the milk. Bring to the boil, remove from the heat and leave to infuse for 30 minutes. Soak the gelatine in 2 tablespoons liqueur until spongy.
2 Strain the milk through a nylon sieve lined with muslin. Return to the pan and bring back to the boil. Whisk the egg yolks with 60g (2oz/¼ cup) of the sugar until thick and light. Stir in a little of the boiling milk, then add to the milk in the pan and cook, stirring, until thick enough to coat the back of the spoon; do not boil.
3 Add the soaked gelatine to the hot custard and stir until dissolved. Cool until beginning to set.
4 Dip the apricots in boiling water for a few seconds to loosen the skins, then peel. Halve and cut into slices. Soak the apricots and ratafias in the remaining liqueur.
5 Whip the cream until soft peaks form, then fold into the cold custard. Stiffly whisk the egg whites, add the remaining 1 tablespoon sugar and fold into the custard. Carefully spoon just over half of this mixture into the prepared ramekins. Chill in the refrigerator until set.
6 Divide the apricot mixture between the ramekins and fill with the remaining soufflé mixture. Chill until set.
7 Carefully remove the paper collars and smooth the sides of the soufflés with a hot knife. Decorate the soufflés with piped cream and apricot slices. **Serves 6**

PRALINE CHARLOTTE

Reserve this elegant dessert for special occasions. Prepare it ahead if you wish, but decorate just before serving otherwise the praline topping will become soft.

Praline:

90g (3oz/⅓ cup) caster sugar · 3 tablespoons water
90g (3oz/½ cup) blanched almonds, toasted

Custard:

7g (¼oz/2½ teaspoons) powdered gelatine
250ml (8 fl oz/1 cup) milk · 1 vanilla pod, split
3 egg yolks · 2 teaspoons caster sugar
250ml (8 fl oz/1 cup) whipping cream

To Finish:

1 packet of sponge fingers · 60g (2oz/¼ cup) caster sugar · 60ml (2 fl oz/¼ cup) water · 2 tablespoons brandy · whipped cream

1 To make the praline, place the sugar and water in a small pan and heat gently until dissolved. Bring to the boil and cook to a golden caramel, then quickly add the almonds. Pour the praline on to an oiled baking sheet. Leave to cool, then grind to a coarse, crunchy texture.
2 Soak the gelatine in 2 teaspoons water. Place the milk in a small pan with the vanilla pod and bring to the boil. Whisk the egg yolks with the sugar until thick and light. Stir in a little of the hot milk, then add to the remaining milk in the pan and cook until thickened enough to lightly coat the back of the spoon; do not boil. Discard the vanilla pod. Add the soaked gelatine and stir; it should dissolve immediately. Chill until on the point of setting, then fold in all but 1 tablespoon praline. Whip cream until soft peaks form, then fold into the custard.
3 Lay the biscuits sugary side down on the work surface. Place the sugar, water and brandy in a small pan and bring slowly to the boil. Moisten each biscuit with a little syrup. Use to line the sides of a 625ml (1 pint/2½ cup) soufflé dish, spooning in a little mousse to help them stand. Pour in the mousse and chill until set.
4 When the charlotte is set, trim the biscuits to the level of the mousse. Dip the soufflé dish into hot water for a few seconds, invert on to a chilled plate and shake to turn the charlotte out. Decorate with piped cream and the remaining praline. **Serves 6**

CHESTNUT BAVARIOS

This light bavarious makes the perfect alternative Christmas dessert. It can be made a day in advance, then turned out and decorated the following day.

7g (¼oz/2½ teaspoons) powdered gelatine
250ml (8 fl oz/1 cup) milk · 250g (8oz) can unsweetened chestnut purée · 3 egg yolks
90g (3oz/⅓ cup) caster sugar · 250ml (8 fl oz/ 1 cup) whipping cream

To Decorate:
whipping cream · 3 marrons glacés, halved
icing sugar for dusting

1 Chill a 940ml (1½ pint/3¾ cup) charlotte tin. Soak the gelatine in 1 tablespoon water until spongy. Place the milk and half of the chestnut purée in a pan and bring to the boil. Whisk together the egg yolks and 60g (2oz/¼ cup) of the sugar until thick and light. Stir in a little of the hot milk, then add to the remaining milk in the pan and cook, stirring, until the custard thickens enough to coat the back of the spoon. Do not allow to boil.

2 Add the soaked gelatine to the hot custard; it should dissolve immediately. Chill until on the point of setting.

3 Whip the cream until soft peaks form and set aside. Place the remaining chestnut purée in a small bowl and break up with a fork. Add the remaining sugar and beat until smooth. Fold in 2 tablespoons of the chilled custard and 1 tablespoon of the cream. Set aside.

4 Fold the remaining cream into the chilled custard and pour half of this bavarois mixture into the charlotte tin. Refrigerate until set. Spoon the chestnut purée on to the set bavarios and spread evenly. Top with the remaining bavarois mixture and chill until set.

5 To unmould the bavarois, run the point of a knife around the top edge. Dip the mould into hot water for a few seconds, then invert on to a chilled plate. Decorate with whirls of cream and marrons glacés. Dust with icing sugar.

Serves 6

FRUIT-FILLED SAVARINS

These pretty individual savarins can be filled with any type of fruit. Try a mixture of soft fruits, such as raspberries, blueberries and strawberry slices.

90g (3oz/¾ cup) strong white flour · pinch of salt 3 tablespoons milk · 7g (¼ oz/1 ½ teaspoons) fresh yeast, or 1 teaspoon dried · 1 teaspoon caster sugar · 1 egg, lightly beaten · 45g (1 ½ oz) butter

Syrup:
90g (3oz/⅓ cup) caster sugar · 155ml (5 fl oz/ ⅔ cup) water · pared rind of 1 lemon · few drops of lemon juice · 1 tablespoon framboise liqueur

To Serve:
250g (8oz) raspberries · mint leaves

1 Grease 4 individual 10cm (4 inch) ring moulds.
2 Sift the flour and salt into a large bowl and make a well in the centre. Heat the milk until lukewarm, then mix in the yeast and sugar. Add the egg to the milk, then pour into the well in the flour. Sprinkle a little of the flour over the liquid and leave to stand in a warm place for 15-20 minutes or until the yeast starts to bubble.
3 Melt the butter and cool slightly before adding to the liquid ingredients. Using a wooden spatula, mix all the ingredients together. Continue beating with the spoon or by hand until a slack, glossy dough is formed. Pour into the prepared moulds and allow to stand in a warm place for 1 hour or until doubled in size.
4 Preheat oven to 200C (400F/Gas 6). Bake savarins for 10-15 minutes or until an inserted skewer comes out clean. Turn out on to a wire rack; leave to cool.
5 To make the syrup, heat the sugar and water gently in a small pan to dissolve the sugar. Add the lemon rind and juice, bring to the boil and cook for 1 minute. Remove from the heat and add the liqueur.
6 Immerse the savarins in the syrup, one at a time, then return to the wire rack placed over a tray to collect any drips. Dab any remaining syrup over the savarins.
7 Place the savarins on individual plates and fill with raspberries. Decorate with mint leaves and serve with pouring cream. **Serves 4**

WILD STRAWBERRY SHORTCAKES

Miniature wild strawberries – *fraise de bois* – are simply delicious. They may be expensive, but a few go a long way in this dessert and the taste sensation is well worth the cost.

Almond Pastry:

250g (8oz/2 cups) plain flour · pinch of salt · 30g (1oz/1/4 cup) ground almonds · 140g (4 1/2oz) butter 100g (3 1/2oz/2/3 cup) icing sugar · 2 egg yolks 2 drops of almond essence

Strawberry Coulis:

375g (12oz) strawberries · 1-2 tablespoons icing sugar · juice of 1/2 lemon (approximately)

To Finish:

375g (12oz) wild strawberries
200ml (6 fl oz/3/4 cup) double (thick) cream
1 tablespoon icing sugar

1 Prepare the almond pastry as for passion fruit tartlets (page 187), adding the ground almonds with the flour, using icing sugar instead of caster sugar and omitting the water. Wrap in plastic wrap and chill for 30 minutes.

2 Preheat the oven to 190C (375F/Gas 5). Roll out the pastry thinly on a lightly floured surface. Using a 10cm (4 inch) fluted pastry cutter, cut out 12 rounds. Place on baking sheets and bake for 7-8 minutes until pale golden. Using a palette knife, transfer the pastry rounds to a wire rack to cool.

3 For the coulis, pureé the hulled strawberries in a blender or food processor. Add icing sugar and lemon juice to taste.

4 Reserve 4 wild strawberries with leaves for decoration; hull the remainder and set aside. Whip the cream with the icing sugar until soft peaks form.

5 To assemble the shortcakes: pipe cream on to 4 biscuits, top each with another biscuit and cover with a layer of wild strawberries and a spoonful of coulis. Dust remaining biscuits with icing sugar and place one on each shortcake.

6 Pour the remaining strawberry coulis on to individual serving plates and place a shortcake in the centre of each. Decorate with the reserved strawberries and leaves. Serve immediately. **Serves 4**

SUMMER FRUIT TARTLETS

Delicate tartlets filled with vanilla-scented pastry cream and piled high with summer fruits. Select seasonal fruits when they are at their best and most flavoursome.

500g (1lb) summer fruits, e.g. strawberries, blackberries, blueberries; black, red and white currants; figs, cape gooseberries

Sweet Pastry:

125g (4oz/1 cup) plain flour · 15g (½oz/ 2 tablespoons) ground almonds · pinch of salt 60g (2oz) butter · 60g (2oz/⅓ cup) icing sugar 1 egg yolk · 1 drop of almond essence

Crème Patissière:

250ml (8 fl oz/1 cup) milk · 1 vanilla pod, split 3 egg yolks · 45g (1½oz/scant ¼ cup) caster sugar 45g (1½oz/¼ cup) plain flour · knob of butter

To Glaze:

3 tablespoons apricot jam, sieved
1 tablespoon water

1 Make the pastry as for passion fruit tartlets (page 187), adding the ground almonds with the flour, using icing sugar instead of caster sugar, and omitting the water.

2 Preheat the oven to 180C (350F/Gas 4). Roll out the pastry thinly and use to line four 10cm (4 inch) tartlet tins. Prick the bases with a fork. Line with greaseproof paper and dried beans. Bake blind for 10 minutes, then remove the beans and paper and cook for 5 minutes. Cool, then remove from the tins.

3 To make the crème patissière, place the milk in a saucepan with the vanilla pod and bring to the boil. In a bowl, whisk the egg yolks and sugar together until pale and thick, then stir in the flour. Pour a little of the hot milk on to the whisked mixture, then add to the milk in the pan. Bring to the boil and cook, stirring, for 2-3 minutes until thickened. Transfer the crème patissière to a plate to cool, dabbing the top with butter to prevent a skin from forming. Discard the vanilla pod.

4 Prepare the fruits: pick over the berries and currants; halve the larger strawberries; cut the figs into wedges; open up the cape gooseberries.

5 Divide the crème patissière between the 4 tartlet cases, spreading it evenly, and arrange the fruits on top. Warm the apricot jam with the water and brush over the fruits to glaze. **Serves 4**

PASSION FRUIT TARTLETS

Passion fruit curd makes a pleasant change from lemon curd and it is just as simple to prepare.

125g (4oz/1 cup) plain flour · pinch of salt 60g (2oz) butter, in pieces · 45g (1 ½oz/scant ¼ cup) caster sugar · 1 egg yolk · 2 teaspoons water · 1 drop of almond essence

Passion Fruit Curd:
4 passion fruit · 125g (4oz/½ cup) caster sugar 125g (4oz) butter · 3 eggs, beaten · 1-2 teaspoons lemon juice

To Decorate:
1 passion fruit

1 To make the pastry, sift the flour and salt into a large bowl. Rub in the butter using the fingertips until the mixture resembles fine breadcrumbs. Stir in the sugar. Mix together the egg yolk, water and almond essence and add to the flour. Stir with a round-bladed knife until the dough clings together. Turn on to a lightly floured surface and knead gently until smooth. Wrap in plastic wrap and chill for 30 minutes.
2 Preheat the oven to 180C (350F/Gas 4). Roll out the pastry thinly and use to line four 10cm (4 inch) tartlet tins. Prick the bases with a fork. Line with greaseproof paper and dried beans. Bake blind for 10 minutes, then remove the baking beans and paper and bake for a further 5 minutes until the pastry is dry. Allow to cool, then remove from the tins.
3 To make the fruit curd, halve the passion fruit and scoop the pulp into a heatproof bowl. Add the sugar and butter. Stand the bowl over a pan of simmering water and stir until the sugar has dissolved. Add the beaten eggs and cook, stirring for 7-8 minutes until the mixture thickens. Sieve and allow to cool slightly. Add lemon juice to taste. Divide the passion fruit curd between the tartlet cases. Leave to set.
4 To serve, halve the remaining passion fruit and spoon a little pulp on to each tartlet. **Serves 4**

CHOCOLATE TRUFFLE PIE

This one is for all the chocoholics I know. Once tasted, never forgotten! For the pie you will only need to use one of the cake layers, so freeze the other one for another occasion.

60g (2oz/½ cup) plain flour
30g (1oz/¼ cup) cocoa powder · 3 eggs
90g (3oz/⅓ cup) caster sugar

Syrup:
60g (2oz/¼ cup) caster sugar · 100ml (3½ fl oz/ ½ cup) water · 1 tablespoon grand marnier

Topping:
470g (15oz) plain (dark) chocolate, in pieces
470ml (15 fl oz/1¾ cups) whipping cream
cocoa powder for dusting

1 Preheat the oven to 180C (350F/Gas 4). Grease the base and side of a 25cm (10 inch) spring form cake tin and line the base with greaseproof paper. Dust the tin with a little flour. Sift together the flour and cocoa.
2 Whisk the eggs and sugar in a large bowl over a pan of hot water using an electric whisk or a large balloon whisk until the mixture is very thick and has trebled in volume. Remove from the heat and whisk until cool. Lightly fold in the flour and cocoa; do not over-mix. Pour the mixture into the prepared tin and bake for 20 minutes until a skewer inserted in the centre comes out clean. Turn out and cool on a wire rack.
3 To make the syrup, put the ingredients in a small pan, bring slowly to the boil and simmer for 1 minute. Cool.
4 Slice the cake in half horizontally. Place one layer, cut side up, in the cake tin and moisten with the syrup.
5 To make the topping, melt the chocolate in a bowl over a pan of hot water. Whisk the cream until it begins to leave a ribbon, pour in the melted chocolate and whisk to mix; do not over-whisk. Pour into the cake tin, smooth the top and chill for 2 hours.
6 Run a warm knife around the pie, then remove the tin. Dust the top with cocoa. **Serves 8-10**

BAKED AMERICAN CHEESECAKE

Personally, I prefer baked cheesecakes to the uncooked variety set with gelatine. For maximum flavour, allow this one to mellow overnight in the refrigerator before serving.

Base:
125g (4oz) ginger biscuits · 60g (2oz) butter

Fillling:
250g (8oz/1 cup) curd cheese · 250g (8oz/1 cup) cream cheese · 3 eggs · 185g (6oz/¾ cup) caster sugar · grated rind of 1 lemon · 30g (1oz/¼ cup) plain flour · 155ml (5 fl oz/⅔ cup) soured cream 100ml (3½ fl oz/scant ½ cup) whipping cream 2 tablespoons seedless raisins, soaked in 2 tablespoons brandy

Topping:
2 lemons · 2 tablespoons honey · 2 tablespoons water · 2.5cm (1 inch) piece fresh root (green) ginger, sliced

1 Preheat the oven to 180C (350F/Gas 4). Lightly grease a 20cm (8 inch) springform tin. Place the biscuits in a plastic bag and crush them with a rolling pin. Melt the butter in a small pan and stir in the crumbs. Press the crumbs on to the base of the prepared tin, spreading them evenly with the back of a spoon. Set aside.
2 In a large bowl, mix together the curd cheese, cream cheese and eggs. Beat in the sugar and lemon rind. Fold in the flour, both creams and the raisins, with 1 tablespoon of the brandy. Spread over the base and bake for 45 minutes. Leave to cool in the switched-off oven for 30 minutes.
3 Score the lemons from top to bottom with a canelle knife, then slice thinly. Place in a pan with the honey, water and ginger. Cover with a disc of greaseproof paper and cook very gently for 20 minutes, until tender.
4 Drain the lemon slices, reserving the liquid and arrange around the edge of the cheesecake. Reduce reserved liquid until syrupy, strain and lightly brush over the lemon slices and top of the cheesecake. Refrigerate overnight. Remove from tin to serve. **Serves 8**

RHUBARB OAT CRUMBLE

The inclusion of oats in the crumble topping adds texture to this traditional pudding. Serve hot or cold, with custard or cream.

1kg (2lb) rhubarb · 185g (6oz/¾ cup) caster sugar grated rind and juice of 1 orange

Topping:
60g (2oz/½ cup) plain flour · 2 teaspoons ground mixed spice · 30g (1oz/¼ cup) ground almonds 90g (3oz/1 cup) rolled oats · 125g (4oz/¾ cup) moist light brown sugar · 125g (4oz) butter, in pieces

1 Preheat the oven to 190C (375F/Gas 5). Cut the rhubarb into 2.5cm (1 inch) batons. Place in a pan with the sugar, orange rind and juice, and cook gently for 5 minutes.
2 To make the topping, in a bowl, mix together the flour, spice, almonds, oats and sugar. Rub in the butter.
3 Place the rhubarb in a 1.25 litre (2 pint/5 cup) ovenproof dish, spoon the crumble mixture evenly over the top and bake for 40 minutes until golden and crisp. Serve with custard or cream. **Serves 6**

MARMALADE & GINGER PUDDING

Few can resist the temptation of a sticky, steamed pudding. Although it is very simple to make you need to allow plenty of time for steaming.

155g (5 oz) butter · 155g (5oz/2/3 cup) caster sugar
2 eggs, lightly beaten · 155g (5oz/1 1/4 cups) self-raising flour · 2 teaspoons ground ginger
2 tablespoons milk (approximately)
250g (8oz/3/4 cup) marmalade

Topping:
2 tablespoons marmalade · juice of 1 orange

1 Grease a 1.25 litre (2 pint/5 cup) pudding basin. In a bowl, cream the butter and sugar together until light and fluffy. Add the eggs, a little at a time, beating well between each addition. Sift the flour and ginger together and fold in, adding enough milk to give a firm dropping consistency.

2 Place the marmalade in the pudding basin and spoon the sponge mixture on top. Cover the basin with a double layer of buttered greaseproof paper or foil and tie securely with string. Put the basin in the top of a steamer (see note). Cover and steam for 1 1/2-1 3/4 hours.

3 Warm the marmalade and orange juice in a small pan. Turn the pudding out on to a warmed dish and pour the sauce over the top.

Serves 6

NOTE: If you do not have a steamer, put the basin into a large saucepan containing enough boiling water to come one third of the way up the basin. Cover and boil steadily for about 1 1/2 hours, topping up with boiling water as necessary.

STICKY TOFFEE PUDDING

This delicious pudding tastes equally good hot or cold. I usually serve it hot as a dessert and save any leftovers for tea the next day.

250g (8oz/1 ½ cups) dates, stoned and chopped
1 teaspoon bicarbonate of soda · 315ml (10 fl oz/ 1 ¼ cups) boiling water · 185g (6oz) butter
185g (6oz/1 cup) soft brown sugar · 1 egg, lightly beaten · 250g (8oz/2 cups) self-raising flour
2 drops of vanilla essence

Walnut Topping:
30g (1 oz) butter · 5 tablespoons soft brown sugar
5 tablespoons double (thick) cream
60g (2oz/½ cup) walnuts, roughly chopped

1 Preheat the oven to 180C (350F/Gas 4). Grease a 1kg (2lb) loaf tin and line with greaseproof paper, leaving at least 2.5cm (1 inch) overlapping all around (to make it easier to remove the pudding after cooking). Place the dates and bicarbonate of soda in a bowl, pour on the boiling water and allow to stand for 20 minutes.
2 In a bowl, cream the butter and sugar together until fluffy. Add the egg, a little at a time, beating well between each addition. Fold in the flour, vanilla essence and the dates together with their liquid; the batter should be quite runny.
3 Pour the mixture into the prepared tin and bake in the oven for 1 hour until cooked but still moist. If the top appears to be browning too quickly during cooking, cover with foil.
4 For the topping, place the butter, brown sugar and cream in a small pan, bring to the boil and simmer gently for 1 minute. Add the walnuts and keep warm.
5 Carefully lift the cooked pudding out of the tin and place on a warmed serving plate. Remove the paper. Pour the walnut topping over to serve. **Serves 8-10**

STEAMED CHOCOLATE PUDDING

Adding the walnuts gives this deliciously moist pudding an interesting texture. Remember to keep the steamer topped up with water during cooking.

125g (4oz) plain (dark) chocolate · 1 tablespoon milk · 125g (4oz) butter · 125g (4oz/¾ cup) soft brown sugar · 2 eggs, lightly beaten · 90 g (3 oz/ ¾ cup) self-raising flour · 60g (2oz/1 cup) fresh breadcrumbs · 30g (1oz/¼ cup) walnuts, chopped

1 Lightly butter a 1.25 litre (2 pint/5 cup) pudding basin. Melt the chocolate together with the milk in a small bowl over a pan of hot water.

2 In a bowl, cream the butter and sugar together until light and fluffy. Add the eggs, a little at a time, beating well between each addition. Fold in the melted chocolate, flour, breadcrumbs and chopped walnuts, using a metal spoon.

3 Spoon the mixture into the pudding basin, cover with a double layer of buttered greaseproof paper or foil and tie securely with string. Put the basin in the top of a steamer (see note). Cover and steam for 1¾ hours, topping up the boiling water as necessary.

4 Remove the paper or foil and turn out the pudding on to a warmed serving plate. Serve hot, with pouring cream or custard. **Serves 6**

NOTE: If you do not have a steamer, put the basin into a large saucepan containing enough boiling water to come one third of the way up the basin. Cover and boil steadily for about 1½ hours, topping up with boiling water as necessary.

APPLE & BLACKBERRY FILO PIE

Filo is one of the easiest pastries to use as it doesn't require rolling out. Here it makes a welcome change from shortcrust pastry to encase a pie filling. My recipe suggests making a large pie, but you could try making individual ones if you prefer.

1kg (2lb) cooking apples · juice of 1 lemon 185g (6oz) butter · 60g (2oz/⅓ cup) moist brown sugar · 10 sheets filo pastry, measuring 36 × 18cm (14 × 7 inches) · 500g (1lb) blackberries

To Finish:
icing sugar for dusting

1 Preheat the oven to 190C (375F/Gas 5). Butter a 20cm (8 inch) loose-bottomed shallow flan tin. Peel, core and slice the apples and toss in a little lemon juice. Melt 30g (1oz) of the butter in a large sauté pan until sizzling. Add the apples and sprinkle with the sugar. Cook over moderate heat until the apples are just beginning to soften, then turn on to a plate to cool.
2 Melt the remaining butter in a small pan. Brush 1 sheet of filo pastry with melted butter, fold in half and brush again with butter. Lay the filo sheet in the prepared dish so that a corner is at the centre of the dish and the filo overlaps the rim generously on that side. Butter and fold each filo sheet before laying in the tin, overlapping the previous sheet as well as the side of the tin. When you have finished the base should be completely covered and there will be a good overlap.
3 Spoon alternate layers of apples and blackberries into the lined tin. Fold the last piece of overlapping filo back over the filling. Repeat with each layer in turn, allowing the filo to form ripples and folds. Brush with a little more butter and dust lightly with icing sugar.
4 Bake for 45 minutes or until the pastry is crisp and golden brown. Serve dusted with icing sugar. **Serves 8**

SUMMER PUDDINGS

Individual versions of the classic summer pudding look most attractive. Use ramekins or oval moulds if you have some.

1 medium cooking apple · grated rind and juice of 1 lemon · 750g (1 ½lb) mixed soft fruits, eg raspberries, redcurrants, blackcurrants, blackberries, strawberries · 185g (6oz/¾ cup) caster sugar · 16 thin slices white bread, crusts removed

To Decorate:
soft fruits and leaves

1 Peel, core and slice the apple and place in a pan with the lemon rind and juice. Cook gently for about 2-3 minutes until the apple slices are just tender but holding their shape.

2 Prepare the soft fruits, removing the stems and stalks; slice the strawberries. Add the soft fruits to the pan with the sugar and cook gently for about 10 minutes, until the sugar has dissolved and the fruit juices are beginning to run. Remove from the heat.

3 Have ready 6 ramekins or other individual moulds. Measure their inside diameter and, using the same-sized pastry cutter, cut out 12 discs of bread. Press one on to the base of each mould. Cut the remaining bread into strips and use to line the sides.

4 Spoon a little juice from the fruit over the bread in the moulds to give a good red colour. Using a slotted spoon, fill them with the fruit and spoon over a little more juice. Top each with another bread round and a spoonful of juice. Strain and reserve the remaining juice.

5 Stand the moulds in a tray, cover with plastic wrap and weigh down each pudding to compress it slightly. Refrigerate overnight.

6 To turn out the puddings, run a small knife around the inside of each dish and invert on to a serving plate. Spoon over the reserved juice and decorate with fruit and leaves. Serve with pouring cream. **Serves 6**

FIG GRATIN

A simple yet sophisticated dessert. Accompany with a glass of chilled Champagne for the perfect end to a summer meal.

6 ripe figs · 3 egg yolks · 1 tablespoon honey
3 tablespoons white wine · 315ml (10 fl oz/1 1/4 cups) whipping cream · 155ml (5 fl oz/2/3 cup) port

To Finish:
icing sugar for dusting

1 Preheat the grill to high and lightly butter 6 heatproof plates. Peel the figs and cut each one into 8 wedges. Arrange on individual plates.

2 Place the egg yolks, honey and white wine in a large heatproof bowl and whisk until evenly mixed. Place the bowl over a pan of boiling water and continue to whisk until the mixture is thick enough to leave a ribbon when the whisk is lifted. Remove the bowl from the heat and whisk until cool.

3 Whisk the cream lightly until it is almost thick enough to leave a ribbon, then fold into the egg mixture together with the port, being careful to avoid over-mixing.

4 Spoon this mixture over the figs as evenly as possible and place each plate under the grill for about 1 minute until golden brown. Dust with a little icing sugar and serve immediately.

Serves 6

NOTE: If the figs are under-ripe, it may be necessary to poach them in a little sugar syrup before assembling the gratin.

SUMMER FRUIT MERINGUE NESTS

To ensure the cream and chocolate sauce ripple to maximum effect they must have the same consistency; if necessary whip the cream slightly.

Meringue Nests:
2 egg whites · pinch of salt
125g (4oz/½ cup) caster sugar

Chocolate Sauce:
155ml (5 fl oz/⅔ cup) milk · 100g (3½ oz) dark chocolate · 15g (½ oz) butter

To Finish:
155ml (5 fl oz/⅔ cup) whipping cream
250g (8oz) raspberries · 250g (8oz) redcurrants

1 Preheat the oven to 120C (250F/Gas ½). Line 2 baking trays with non-stick paper and mark two 10cm (4 inch) circles on each.

2 In a large grease-free bowl, whisk the egg whites with the salt until stiff peaks form. Add half of the sugar a spoonful at a time, whisking well between each addition. Carefully fold in the remaining sugar, using a spatula, to give a very stiff and glossy meringue.

3 Transfer the meringue to a piping bag fitted with a 1cm (½ inch) fluted nozzle. Pipe over each marked circle, starting at the centre and working outwards in a spiral. Pipe 1 or 2 more layers around the edge.

4 Bake in the oven for 2 hours or until firm. Transfer to a wire rack and allow to cool.

5 To make the chocolate sauce, pour the milk into a small pan and bring to the boil. Remove from the heat, add the chocolate, let stand for 2 minutes, then stir until smooth. Add the butter and set aside to cool.

6 Pour a pool of cream on to each individual plate. Drizzle the chocolate sauce around the edge and work with a skewer to give a rippled effect. Stand the meringue nests on top and fill with raspberries and redcurrants. Serve immediately. **Serves 4**

PEARS WITH FIGS & POMEGRANATE

An ideal dessert for winter, featuring delicious fruits in a warming spicy syrup. A good robust red wine, such as St Emillion, is perfect for the syrup.

6 pears · 3 figs · 2 seedless oranges · 1 pomegranate

Wine Syrup:
2 bottles red wine · 1 cinnamon stick · 4 cloves
4 green cardamom pods · 1 bay leaf · 1 star anise
2 coriander seeds · 2 white peppercorns
1 cm (1/2 inch) cube fresh root (green) ginger, thinly sliced · 90g (3oz/1/3 cup) soft brown sugar

1 To make the syrup, pour the wine into a large saucepan, bring to the boil and simmer, uncovered, until reduced by one third. Tie the spices in a square of muslin and add to the wine with the ginger and sugar. Continue to simmer until the liquid is reduced to half of its original volume.
2 Peel and halve the pears, then scoop out the cores, using a melon baller. Add them to the wine, cover with a disc of greaseproof paper and simmer for 15-20 minutes until the pears are tender. Quarter the figs, add to the hot syrup and leave to cool, so they absorb the flavours.
3 Peel and segment the oranges. Halve the pomegranate and scoop out the flesh.
4 Lift the pears and figs out of the syrup and place in a glass serving bowl. Add the orange segments and pomegranate flesh. Strain the syrup; taste and add a little more sugar if necessary. Pour the syrup over the fruit to serve. **Serves 6**

SUMMER FRUIT SALAD

Serve this dessert to refresh the palate at the end of a meal. Select fruits with flavours and colours which complement one another. Ensure they are fully ripe so there is no need to add sugar.

Fruits in Season:
2 kiwi fruit · 1 papaya · 1 star fruit · 2 nectarines 125g (4oz) raspberries · 8 strawberries · 2 passion fruit (optional)

Mango Sauce:
1 large ripe mango · 1 tablespoon lemon juice 1 tablespoon honey

To Decorate:
mint sprigs

1 First make the mango sauce. Peel and roughly chop the mango, discarding the stone. Place in a blender or food processor with the lemon juice and honey and work to a smooth purée; set aside.

2 To prepare the fruits, peel and slice the kiwi fruit and papaya. Slice the star fruit and nectarines. Pick over the raspberries; halve the strawberries but do not hull. Halve the passion fruit, if using, and scoop out the flesh.

3 Spoon a pool of mango purée on to each dessert plate and arrange the fruits attractively on top. Decorate with mint sprigs to serve. **Serves 4**

ICED CHOCOLATE TERRINE

When melting chocolate over a bain marie, or a pan of hot water, it is important that the temperature of the chocolate does not exceed 35C (85F) otherwise it will spoil.

60g (2oz/1/3 cup) prunes, pitted · 60g (2oz/1/3 cup) dates, pitted · 60ml (2 fl oz/1/4 cup) brandy · 100ml (3 1/2 fl oz/1/4 cup) hot black tea · 315ml (10 fl oz/ 1 1/4 cups) double (thick) cream · 375g (12oz) plain (dark) chocolate · 90g (3oz) butter · 3 egg yolks 2 egg whites · 2 teaspoons caster sugar

To Decorate:

2-3 plums, stoned and sliced

1 Put the prunes and dates in a bowl. Pour the brandy and tea over them, stir and leave to soak overnight.

2 Drain the fruits and chop roughly; reserve the liquor.

3 Whip half of the cream until soft peaks form and spread evenly over the base and sides of a 940ml (1 1/2 pint/3 3/4 cup) terrine. Place in the freezer until firm.

4 Melt the chocolate and butter in a heatproof bowl over a pan of hot water. Stir in the egg yolks, soaked fruit and about half of the reserved liquor; the mixture should be fairly stiff.

5 Whip the remaining cream until it forms soft peaks. In another bowl, whisk the egg whites until stiff, then add the sugar, whisking constantly until glossy peaks form. Stir a spoonful of the cream into the chocolate mixture to lighten it. Fold in the remaining cream, then fold in the egg whites.

6 Pour this mixture into the cream-lined terrine, cover with plastic wrap and freeze for 3-4 hours or until firm.

7 To serve, run the point of a knife around the inside of the terrine and dip it briefly in hot water. Invert on to a chilled plate and slice thinly with a sharp knife. Serve decorated with plum slices. **Serves 8-10**

BOMBE TUTTI FRUTTI

For those who don't like the traditional Christmas pudding this is an excellent alternative with a festive flavour. But it can, of course, be served at any time of the year.

Tutti Fruitti Ice Cream:
30g (1 oz/¼ cup) dried apricots · 30g (1 oz/¼ cup) maraschino cherries, drained and chopped 30g (1 oz/¼ cup) raisins · 30g (1 oz/¼ cup) candied fruits, chopped · 2 tablespoons brandy · 2 eggs, separated · 45g (1½oz/6½ tsp) caster sugar 30g (1 oz/¼ cup) flaked almonds · 155ml (5 fl oz/ ⅔ cup) double (thick) cream, softly whipped

Vanilla Ice Cream:
250ml (8fl oz/1 cup) milk · 1 vanilla pod, split 3 egg yolks · 60g (2oz/¼ cup) caster sugar · 250ml (8 fl oz/1 cup) double (thick) cream, softly whipped

To Decorate:
crystallized fruits and angelica diamonds

1 Chill a 940ml (1½ pint/3¾ cup) bombe mould. Soak the apricots in boiling water to cover until well swollen; drain and chop. Place in a bowl with the cherries, raisins, candied fruits and brandy. Leave for several hours or overnight. Drain, reserving 1 teaspoon juice.
2 Whisk the egg whites until stiff, then gradually whisk in the sugar to yield a stiff, glossy meringue. Fold into the whipped cream with the egg yolks, almonds, soaked fruits and reserved juice. Spread the mixture around the base and sides of the bombe mould. Freeze until firm.
3 To make the vanilla ice cream, put the milk in a small pan with the vanilla pod and bring to the boil. Whisk together the egg yolks and sugar until thick and light. Stir in a little of the hot milk, then add to the milk in the pan and cook, stirring, until thick enough to coat the back of the spoon; do not boil. Allow to cool, then discard the vanilla pod.
4 Freeze the custard in a shallow tray until crystals form at the edges; remove from freezer and beat until smooth. Freeze until almost set, beat once more, then fold in the whipped cream and freeze until just firm.
5 Fill the centre of the bombe with the vanilla ice cream, cover and freeze overnight.
6 To serve, quickly dip the bombe into hot water and invert on to a chilled serving plate. Decorate with crystallized fruits and angelica. **Serves 8**

YOGURT & HONEY ICE WITH TUILES

The inspiration for this dish came from sitting in Greek tavernas on sun-baked afternoons eating yogurt drizzled with honey. Experiment with flavoured honeys, such as acacia, lavender or clover.

315ml (10 fl oz/1 ¼ cups) milk · 4 egg yolks 155ml (5 fl oz/⅔ cup) honey · 185ml (6 fl oz/ ¾ cup) Greek yogurt · 315ml (10 fl oz/1 ¼ cups) whipping cream, lightly whipped

Tuiles:
125g (4oz/1 cup) chopped almonds · 30g (1oz/ ¼ cup) plain flour · 125g (4oz/¾ cup) icing sugar 2 drops of orange flower water · 2 egg whites 60g (2oz) butter, melted and cooled

To Serve:
extra honey

1 To make the ice cream, bring the milk to the boil in a saucepan. In a bowl, whisk together the egg yolks and honey until thick and light. Stir a little of the hot milk into the whisked mixture, then add to the milk in the pan and cook over a low heat, stirring constantly, until thick enough to coat the back of the spoon; do not boil. Allow to cool to room temperature.

2 Fold the yogurt and cream into the cooled custard. Pour into an ice cream machine and churn until thick, then transfer to a freezerproof container and freeze until required. Alternatively, pour into a shallow tray and freeze, beating twice during freezing.

3 To make the tuiles, preheat the oven to 200C (400F/ Gas 6) and lightly grease 2 baking sheets. Mix the almonds, flour and icing sugar in a bowl. Add the remaining ingredients and stir until smooth; chill for 10 minutes.

4 Spoon the mixture into mounds on the baking sheets, spacing well apart. Spread into thin rounds. Bake for 5 minutes until pale golden. Allow to cool slightly before carefully lifting them off and laying over a rolling pin. Remove when cold.

5 To serve, scoop the ice cream on to serving plates, drizzle a little honey over the top and serve at once, with the tuiles. **Serves 6**

CINNAMON ICE & CALVADOS APPLES

Apples and cinnamon have always been a great partnership. Here an unusual cinnamon ice cream is perfectly complemented by delectable hot calvados-flavoured apples.

500ml (16 fl oz/2 cups) milk · 6 cinnamon sticks
6 egg yolks · 125g (4oz/½ cup) caster sugar
1 teaspoon ground cinnamon · 250ml (8 fl oz/1 cup) whipping cream, lightly whipped

Calvados Apples:
2 Bramley's or other cooking apples · 30g (1oz) butter · 1-2 teaspoons lemon juice · 30g (1oz/5 teaspoons) caster sugar · dash of calvados

To Serve:
ground cinnamon for sprinkling

1 Place the milk and cinnamon sticks in a small pan and bring to the boil. Beat the egg yolks with the sugar until light, then stir in a little of the hot milk. Add to the milk in the saucepan and cook, stirring constantly, until thickened; do not boil. Allow to cool.

2 Remove the cinnamon sticks from the custard and stir in the ground cinnamon.

3 Transfer to an ice cream machine and churn for 20 minutes, until quite thick. Add the cream and churn for a further 10 minutes or until set. Alternatively, pour the custard into a shallow freezerproof tray and freeze until ice crystals begin to form around the edge; remove from the freezer and beat for 1 minute. Continue freezing, beating twice more until half-set. Turn into a bowl and beat in the cream. Transfer the ice cream to a freezerproof container and freeze until firm.

4 Peel, core and thickly slice the apples. Heat the butter in a frying pan until sizzling. Add the apples, sprinkle with lemon juice and sugar and sauté over a high heat for 2-3 minutes until soft. Add a little calvados and flambé.

5 Scoop the ice cream on to serving plates and surround with the hot apples. Top with a sprinkling of ground cinnamon.

Serves 4

FROZEN STRAWBERRY YOGURT

This recipe can be adapted to suit most soft fruits; try using apricots, mango and even banana too. Although ice creams will keep for several weeks in the freezer, they always taste better a day or two after you make them.

125g (4oz/½ cup) caster sugar · 250ml (8 fl oz/1 cup) water · 500g (1lb) strawberries
315ml (10 fl oz/1¼ cups) thick strawberry yogurt
155ml (5fl oz/⅔ cup) double (thick) cream
1 egg white

1 Put the sugar and water in a saucepan and heat gently until the sugar has dissolved. Bring to the boil and boil steadily until the syrup registers 107C (225F) on a sugar thermometer, or until a little of the syrup forms a thread when pressed between a wet thumb and forefinger and drawn apart.

2 Set aside a few strawberries for decoration; roughly chop a further 60g (2oz). Place the remainder in a blender or food processor with the sugar syrup and work to a purée. Transfer to a bowl and allow to cool. Fold in the yogurt.

3 Transfer the mixture to an ice cream machine and churn until beginning to set. Whip the cream until soft peaks form. In another bowl, whisk the egg white to the same stage. Fold both into the frozen mixture with the chopped strawberries. Continue to churn until firm, then transfer to a freezerproof container and freeze until firm.

4 Alternatively, pour the yogurt and strawberry mixture into a shallow tray and freeze until beginning to set. Transfer to a chilled bowl and beat until smooth. Fold in the whipped cream and whisked egg white and return to the freezer until firm.

5 To serve, scoop into glass serving dishes and decorate with the reserved strawberries. **Serves 6**

LEMON CURD ICE IN BASKETS

Spicy brandy snap baskets are the perfect partner for this tangy lemon ice cream.

Lemon Curd Ice:
6 egg yolks · 2 egg whites · 125g (4oz) butter 315g (10oz/1 1/4 cups) caster sugar · grated rind and juice of 3 lemons · 625ml (20 fl oz/2 1/2 cups) double (thick) cream · 625ml (20 fl oz/2 1/2 cups) Greek yogurt

Candied Lemon Zest:
shredded rind of 1 lemon · 1 tablespoon caster sugar 2 tablespoons water

Brandy Snaps Baskets:
60g (2oz/1/2 cup) plain flour · 1 teaspoon ground ginger · 60g (2oz) butter · 125g (4oz/1/2 cup) caster sugar · 2 tablespoons golden syrup

1 Lightly mix together the egg yolks and whites, strain. Melt the butter in a bowl over a pan of boiling water, add the sugar, eggs and rind and juice of 2 lemons. Stir constantly until the mixture thickens. Allow to cool.

2 Whip the cream until it is the same consistency as the yogurt. Stir a little of each into the lemon curd to lighten it. Fold in the remainder, together with the juice and rind of the remaining lemon. Freeze until required.

3 For the candied lemon zest, put the ingredients in a pan and cook until beginning to caramelize. Cool.

4 Preheat the oven to 200C (400F/Gas 6). Grease 2 large baking sheets and oil 2 oranges (for moulding the brandy snap baskets). Sift together the flour and ginger. Cream the butter until soft and light, then add the sugar, golden syrup and flour. Mix to a smooth dough. Chill for 20 minutes.

5 Form the dough into 8 balls. Place one in the centre of each baking sheet and cook for 8-10 minutes until golden and bubbling. Allow to cool for 1 minute, then carefully remove with a palette knife and place each one over an orange, gently pressing the sides to form folds. Allow to cool before removing. Repeat to make 8 baskets.

6 To serve, fill each basket with lemon ice and top with candied lemon zest and mint, if wished. **Serves 8**

CAKES

There is nothing quite like a homemade cake or gâteau and this varied collection provides you with plenty of recipes to choose from! Ideas range from fresh fruit cakes, with original fillings and toppings, to traditional family favourites and cakes for special occasions.

PECAN & PUMPKIN CAKE

Make use of pumpkins when they are around at Hallowe'en. Teamed with pecan nuts and the subtle flavour of mace, they make an interesting cake. Use other nuts for a change, such as brazils, hazelnuts, pine nuts or walnuts.

500g (1 lb) pumpkin · 125g (4oz) soft margarine 125g (4oz/½ cup) caster sugar · 2 tablespoons clear honey · 2 eggs, beaten · 90g (3oz/½ cup) pecan nuts, chopped · 250g (8oz/2 cups) self-raising flour · 1 teaspoon ground cinnamon

Topping:
2 tablespoons clear honey · ¼ teaspoon ground cinnamon · 8-12 pecan nuts · 2 tablespoons pumpkin seeds

1 Lightly grease and line an 18cm (7 inch) round cake tin. Preheat oven to 160C (325F/Gas 3).
2 Peel the pumpkin, chop roughly and cook in 155ml (5 fl oz/⅔ cup) boiling water for 2-3 minutes until tender; drain well and mash.
3 Beat the margarine, sugar and honey together in a mixing bowl until light and fluffy. Gradually add the eggs, beating well after each addition. Stir in the pumpkin and nuts. Sift the flour and cinnamon together over the mixture, then carefully fold in using a spatula.
4 Place mixture in prepared tin, smooth top and bake in oven for 1 hour 10 minutes to 1 hour 15 minutes, or until the cake springs back when lightly pressed in the centre. Leave to cool in the tin for 5 minutes, then turn out onto a wire rack. Remove the paper, invert the cake and leave until cold.
5 For the topping heat the honey and cinnamon in a small pan, bring to the boil, then remove from heat. Brush the top of the cake with glaze and decorate with pecan nuts and pumpkin seeds. Brush the nuts and seeds with more glaze. **Serves 16**

SPICED APPLE CAKE

When apples are plentiful, combine them with a mixture of spices to make this delicious moist cake. Decorate with red and green apple slices for a tempting top. Pears or plums can be used in place of the apples. Store in a cool place and eat within 2-3 days, or omit the topping and simply glaze with honey to store for up to a week.

250g (8oz) peeled and cored apples, grated · 155g (5 oz) soft margarine · 185g (6oz/¾ cup) caster sugar · 60g (2oz/⅓ cup) currants · 60g (2oz/½ cup) pine nuts · 2 eggs, beaten · 280g (9oz/2¼ cups) plain flour · 1 teaspoon bicarbonate of soda · 1 teaspoon ground cinnamon · 1 teaspoon ground nutmeg · ½ teaspoon ground cloves

Topping:

1 red apple · 1 green apple · 1 tablespoon lemon juice · 2 tablespoons icing sugar, sifted

1 Lightly grease and line an 18cm (7 inch) square cake tin. Preheat oven to 180C (350F/Gas 4).

2 Place the grated apple in a large mixing bowl with the margarine, sugar, currants, pine nuts and egg. Sift in the flour, bicarbonate of soda and spices and mix together with a wooden spoon. Beat for 1-2 minutes until smooth and glossy.

3 Spoon the mixture into the prepared tin, smooth the top and bake in oven for 1 hour 5 minutes to 1 hour 10 minutes, or until the cake springs back when lightly pressed in the centre. Leave in tin for 5 minutes, then turn out onto a wire rack, remove paper and allow to cool.

4 For the topping, cut apples into quarters, remove cores and slice thinly. Toss in lemon juice to prevent discolouring. Arrange apple slices over top of cake, dredge with icing sugar and place under a preheated hot grill for 1-2 minutes until the sugar has caramelized. Leave to cool before serving. **Serves 18**

HARVEST CAKE

A moist, wholesome cake to make when autumnal fruit and nuts are plentiful. It is ideal for keeping or freezing in portions – if you omit the fruit topping and simply glaze with honey.

375g (12oz) plums, stoned and chopped · 500g (1lb) pears, peeled and grated · 375g (12oz/2 cups) raisins · 125g (4oz/¾ cup) hazelnuts, chopped
315g (10 fl oz/1¼ cups) apple juice, warmed
375g (12oz) soft margarine
375g (12oz/2 cups) light soft brown sugar
4 eggs, beaten · 500g (1lb/4 cups) self-raising wholewheat flour · 2 teaspoons ground mixed spice
8 wheat biscuits (eg Weetabix), total weight 185g (6oz), crumbled

Topping:
60ml (2 fl oz/¼ cup) clear honey · 4 wheat biscuits (eg Weetabix), total weight 90g (3oz), crumbled
4 red plums, chopped · 2 pears, chopped
icing sugar for dusting

1 Lightly grease and line a 30 × 23cm (12 × 9 inch) oblong cake tin or roasting tin. Preheat oven to 160C (325F/ Gas 3).
2 Place the plums, pears, raisins, hazelnuts and warmed apple juice in a large mixing bowl. Stir well, cover and leave for several hours or overnight.
3 Place the margarine, sugar, eggs, flour and spice in another bowl, mix together with a wooden spoon, then beat until light and fluffy.
4 Add wheat biscuits to the fruit and mix together, then add the cake mixture and stir until evenly mixed.
5 Spoon mixture into prepared tin and smooth top. Bake in oven for 2½-3 hours, or until cake springs back when pressed in the centre. Leave cake in tin until cold, then turn out, remove paper and invert cake.
6. To make topping, place the honey in a saucepan and bring slowly to the boil. Crumble in the wheat biscuits and stir in the fruit. Spread the mixture evenly over the top of the cake and leave to cool. Dredge with icing sugar to serve.

Serves 48

OATIE BANANA BREAD

A light textured tea loaf made with medium oatmeal, bananas and treacle. You can always use syrup or honey instead of treacle, and vary the nuts if you like.

220g (7oz/1¾ cups) self-raising flour · 1 teaspoon baking powder · 90g (3oz/⅔ cup) medium oatmeal 60g (2oz/⅓ cup) dark soft brown sugar 125g (4oz) soft margarine · 90g (3oz/¼ cup) black treacle · 60g (2oz/⅔ cup) walnuts, chopped 2 bananas, mashed · 1 egg · 6 tablespoons milk

Topping:
1 tablespoon black treacle, melted · 16 dried banana slices · 8 walnut halves

1 Lightly grease and line a 1kg (2lb) loaf tin. Preheat oven to 160C (325F/Gas 3).

2 Sift the flour and baking powder into a large mixing bowl; add the oatmeal, sugar, margarine, black treacle, walnuts, bananas, egg and milk. Mix together with a wooden spoon, then beat for 1-2 minutes until smooth and glossy.

3 Place the mixture in the prepared tin, smooth top and bake in oven for 1 hour 15 minutes to 1 hour 20 minutes, or until the cake springs back when lightly pressed in the centre. Turn out onto a wire rack, remove paper, invert cake and leave until cold.

4 Brush top of cake with warm treacle and decorate with banana slices and walnuts. **Serves 14**

DANISH PLUM CAKE

A plain cake with a moist, spiced fruit centre. Ground mace, allspice or nutmeg can be used as an alternative to cinnamon. With its fresh fruit topping and filling, this cake should be stored in a cool place and eaten within 2 days.

125g (4oz) butter, softened · 125g (4oz/½ cup) caster sugar · 1 egg · 250g (8oz/2 cups) self-raising flour · 3 tablespoons milk

Filling:
375g (12oz) plums, stoned and sliced · 3 teaspoons caster sugar · 1 teaspoon ground cinnamon

Topping:
4 plums, stoned and sliced · 1 tablespoon plum jam, melted

To Finish:
icing sugar and ground cinnamon for dusting

1 Lightly grease and flour an 18cm (7 inch) ring tin. Preheat oven to 180C (350F/Gas 4).
2 Beat the butter and sugar together in a bowl, add the egg and beat thoroughly. Fold in the flour and milk carefully using a spatula until all flour is incorporated.
3 Spoon half of the mixture into prepared tin and smooth the surface. Arrange plum slices over the mixture and sprinkle evenly with sugar and cinnamon. Cover with the remaining mixture and smooth the surface.
4 Bake in oven for 1 hour to 1 hour 10 minutes, or until the cake springs back when pressed in the centre. Loosen the edges with a knife, turn out onto a wire rack and leave to cool.
5 For the topping, arrange the remaining plum slices around the top of the cake and brush with melted jam. Dust the cake completely with icing sugar sifted with cinnamon. **Serves 16**

VARIATION: Use greengages, damsons, cherries, apples or pears in place of the plums.

STICKY GINGER CAKE

A really moist cake with good keeping qualities, topped with a tangy orange butter icing. For a spice cake, replace the ginger with mixed spice and flavour the icing with lemon or lime.

125g (4oz/4 tablespoons) golden syrup · 125g (4oz/4 tablespoons) black treacle · 140ml (4½ fl oz/7 tablespoons) sunflower oil · 125g (4oz/¾ cup) light soft brown sugar · 125ml (4 fl oz/½ cup) milk 250g (8oz/2 cups) plain flour · 3 teaspoons ground ginger · 1 egg, beaten · ½ teaspoon bicarbonate of soda

Orange Butter Icing:
90g (3oz) unsalted butter, softened · 3 teaspoons finely grated orange rind · 4 teaspoons orange juice 185g (6oz/1 cup) icing sugar, sifted

To Decorate:
3 pieces crystallized ginger, thinly sliced

1 Lightly grease and line a 20cm (8in) square cake tin. Preheat oven to 150C (300F/Gas 2).
2 Measure the golden syrup, treacle and oil carefully into a saucepan. Add the brown sugar and milk and place over a low heat, stirring occasionally, until melted.
3 Sift the flour and ginger into a bowl and add the egg. Remove pan from heat, stir in the bicarbonate of soda and quickly pour onto the flour mixture. Using a wooden spoon, beat until smooth.
4 Pour mixture into the prepared tin and bake for 60-70 minutes or until the cake springs back when pressed in the centre. Leave in tin for 5 minutes, then turn out onto a wire rack, remove paper, turn cake right way up and leave until cold.
5 To make the orange butter icing, put the butter into a bowl and beat with a wooden spoon until soft. Add the orange rind, juice and icing sugar and beat together until light and fluffy.
6 Spread two thirds of the icing evenly over top of cake, marking icing with lines. Place the remaining icing in a piping bag fitted with a small star nozzle and pipe a border around the edge of the cake. Decorate with crystallized ginger. **Serves 20**

PASSION CAKE

Passion fruit with its intensely flavoured flesh and edible seeds gives the cake its distinctive flavour and unusual texture. If you prefer a smooth texture simply use the juice and discard the seeds.

185g (6oz/1 ½ cups) self-raising flour
1 ½ teaspoons baking powder · 185g (6oz/¾ cup) caster sugar · 185g (6oz) soft margarine
3 eggs, beaten · 2 passion fruit

Passion Fruit Frosting:
3 passion fruit · 60g (2oz) soft margarine
250g (8oz/1 ½ cups) icing sugar, sifted

To Finish:
cocoa powder for dusting

1 Lightly grease and line a 20cm (8 inch) square cake tin. Preheat oven to 160C (325F/Gas 3).

2 Sift the flour and baking powder into a mixing bowl, then add the sugar, margarine and eggs. Mix with a wooden spoon, then beat for 1-2 minutes until smooth and glossy. Cut passion fruit in half, scoop out the flesh and seeds and add to the cake mixture; stir until well blended.

3 Place mixture in prepared tin, smooth top and bake in oven for 40-45 minutes, or until cake springs back when lightly pressed in the centre. Cool in tin for 5 minutes, turn out onto a wire rack, remove paper and turn cake right way up. Leave until cold.

4 To make the passion fruit frosting, halve passion fruit, scoop out flesh and seeds into a nylon sieve over a bowl and press out juice using a wooden spoon. Add the margarine to the bowl and place over a saucepan of simmering water until melted. Add the icing sugar and beat until mixture is smooth and glossy.

5 Place cake on a wire rack over a plate, pour frosting over to cover completely and leave to set. Cut out 12 strips of paper 23 × 1cm (9 × ½ inch) and arrange on top of the cake in a lattice. Sift cocoa over the top of the cake, then carefully remove each paper strip, leaving a neat pattern.

Serves 18-24

CARROT CAKE

A really quick and easy recipe for a deliciously moist cake containing carrots, spices, raisins and honey. To vary the flavour, try cinnamon, nutmeg or mace instead of mixed spice; for a darker cake replace half of the honey with black treacle.

250g (8oz) carrots, finely grated · 125g (4oz/ 3/4 cup) raisins · 60g (2oz/1/3 cup) figs, chopped 125g (4oz/1/2 cup) caster sugar · 125g (4oz) unsalted butter · 185g (6oz/1/2 cup) clear honey 155ml (5 fl oz/2/3 cup) orange juice · 250g (8oz/ 2 cups) self-raising flour · 1 teaspoon ground mixed spice · 1 egg, beaten

Topping:

185g (6oz/1 cup) icing sugar, sifted · 3 teaspoons orange juice · 3 teaspoons grated orange rind 60g (2oz) marzipan · few drops of orange food colouring

1 Lightly grease and base line a 23cm (9 inch) spring form cake tin. Preheat oven to 160C (325F/Gas 3).

2 Put the carrots, raisins, figs, caster sugar, butter, honey and orange juice in a saucepan. Heat gently, stirring occasionally, until the sugar and butter have melted. Transfer to a mixing bowl and allow to cool. Sift the flour and spice together over the mixture, add the egg and beat thoroughly until well blended.

3 Place the mixture in the prepared tin, smooth top and bake in oven for 1 hour to 1 hour 10 minutes, or until the cake springs back when lightly pressed in the centre. Loosen edge with a palette knife, unclip spring to release cake and remove base and paper. Cool on a wire rack.

4 To make the topping, combine the icing sugar and orange juice and beat until smooth. Spread the icing evenly over the top of the cold cake. Knead orange rind and orange colouring into marzipan. Grate on a coarse grater and sprinkle around the top edge of the cake. Leave to set. **Serves 16**

COURGETTE (ZUCCHINI) CAKE

When courgettes (zucchini) are plentiful, this is a good way to use them. This unusual cake, which includes mixed dried fruit and lemon, makes an excellent alternative to a traditional farmhouse fruit cake. It keeps well in a cool place.

250g (8oz) courgettes (zucchini), grated
185g (6oz/1 1/4 cups) mixed dried fruit · 125g (4oz/ 1/3 cup) lemon marmalade · grated rind and juice of 1 lemon · 125g (4oz) butter, softened
125g (4oz/3/4 cup) light soft brown sugar
2 eggs, beaten · 250g (8oz/2 cups) self-raising wholemeal flour

To Decorate:
icing sugar for dusting · 2 teaspoons lemon rind shreds

1 Lightly grease and line a 20cm (8 inch) round cake tin. Preheat oven to 160C (325F/Gas 3).
2 Put the courgettes (zucchini), dried fruit, marmalade, lemon rind and juice into a bowl. Stir until evenly blended. Beat the butter and sugar together in a mixing bowl until light and fluffy. Add the eggs and beat until thoroughly blended. Stir in the courgette (zucchini) mixture, then carefully fold in the flour using a spatula until evenly incorporated.
3 Spoon mixture into prepared tin, smooth top and bake for 1 hour, or until the cake springs back when pressed lightly in the centre. Cool in tin for 5 minutes, then turn out onto a wire rack, remove paper and invert cake. Leave until cold.
4 To decorate, dredge icing sugar liberally and evenly over the top of the cake, then sprinkle the lemon shreds in the centre. **Serves 16-18**

CHOCOLATE FUDGE CAKE

In this scrumptious chocolate cake I have included ground almonds to give a moist, soft texture and covered the cake with a rich frosting.

125g (4oz/1 cup) self-raising flour · 3 tablespoons cocoa powder · 60g (2oz/½ cup) ground almonds 155g (5oz/⅔ cup) caster sugar · 125ml (4 fl oz/ ½ cup) sunflower oil · 3 eggs, separated · 125ml (4 fl oz/½ cup) boiling water

Chocolate Fudge Icing:
125g (4oz) plain (dark) chocolate, in pieces 60g (2oz) unsalted butter · 1 egg, beaten · 185g (6oz/1 cup) icing sugar, sifted

To Decorate:
24 split almonds · 6 mimosa balls

1 Lightly grease and base line two 20cm (8 inch) round sandwich tins. Preheat oven to 160C (325F/Gas 3).
2 Sift the flour and cocoa powder together into a bowl. Stir in the ground almonds and caster sugar; make a well in the centre. Whisk the oil and egg yolks together in a jug, then add to the dry ingredients with the boiling water. Beat to a smooth batter. Stiffly whisk the egg whites, add to the chocolate mixture and fold in carefully using a spatula.
3 Divide the mixture evenly between prepared tins, smooth tops and bake in oven for 20-25 minutes, or until cakes spring back when lightly pressed in the centre. Turn out onto a wire rack to cool.
4 To make the chocolate fudge icing, melt the chocolate and butter in a bowl over a saucepan of hot water. Stir in the egg, then add the icing sugar and beat until smooth.
5 Sandwich the cakes together with a quarter of the icing. Place cake on wire rack over a plate and pour remaining icing over to cover completely. Leave to set. Spoon the icing from the plate into a piping bag fitted with a star nozzle and pipe 8 swirls on top of cake. Decorate with almonds and mimosa balls. **Serves 12**

MOCHA HAZELNUT CAKE

A light hazelnut cake with a subtle coffee flavour, enhanced by a creamy yogurt filling and a mocha topping.

1 tablespoon coffee granules · 3 tablespoons boiling water · 185g (6oz) butter, softened
185g (6oz/¾ cup) caster sugar · 2 eggs, beaten · 185g (6oz/1 ½ cups) self-raising wholemeal flour · 2 teaspoons baking powder
125g (4oz/1 cup) hazelnuts, toasted and chopped

Filling:
155ml (5 fl oz/⅔ cup) double (thick) cream
2 tablespoons Greek yogurt

Topping:
125g (4oz) plain (dark) chocolate, in pieces
1 teaspoon coffee granules · 1 tablespoon boiling water · 1 tablespoon Greek yogurt · 12 hazelnuts

1 Lightly grease and base line two 20cm (8 inch) sandwich tins. Preheat oven to 160C (325F/Gas 3).

2 Dissolve the coffee in the boiling water. Beat the butter and sugar together in a mixing bowl until light and fluffy. Add the eggs gradually, beating well after each addition. Sift the flour and baking powder onto the mixture, add the coffee and hazelnuts and fold in carefully using a spatula.

3 Divide the mixture between prepared tins, smooth tops and bake in oven for 30-35 minutes, or until the cakes spring back when lightly pressed in the centre. Turn out onto a wire rack, remove paper and invert cakes. Leave until cold.

4 To make the filling, whip the cream with the yogurt until thick. Place one third in a piping bag fitted with a star nozzle.

5 To make the topping, melt the chocolate in a bowl over a pan of hot water. Dissolve the coffee in the boiling water; cool. Stir the coffee and yogurt into the chocolate until smooth. Spread one third over the base cake and cover with the cream filling. Position the other cake on top.

6 Cover the top with the remaining chocolate and pipe 12 swirls of cream around edge. Place a hazelnut on each swirl of cream. Leave to set. **Serves 12**

SUMMER LEMON CAKE

A light lemon sponge – kept moist by a lemon crème au beurre icing. Try replacing the lemons with oranges or limes.

3 eggs · 90g (3oz/1/3 cup) caster sugar · 60g (2oz/1/2 cup) plain flour · 30g (1oz/3 tablespoons) cornflour · 30g (1oz) unsalted butter, melted 2 teaspoons grated lemon rind

Crème au Beurre:
90g (3oz/1/3 cup) caster sugar · 4 tablespoons lemon juice · 2 egg yolks · 155g (5oz) unsalted butter, softened

To Decorate:
lemon rind shreds

1 Lightly grease and line a 20cm (8 inch) round cake tin. Preheat oven to 180C (350F/Gas 4).
2 Place the eggs and sugar in a heatproof bowl over a saucepan of simmering water. Whisk until the mixture becomes thick and pale. Remove bowl from pan and whisk until the mixture leaves a trail on the suface when the beaters are lifted.
3 Sift the flour and cornflour onto the surface of the mixture; add butter and lemon rind. Carefully fold into mixture using a spatula until all flour is incorporated. Pour mixture into prepared tin and bake in oven for 35-40 minutes, or until the cake springs back when pressed in the centre. Turn out onto a wire rack to cool.
4 To make crème au beurre, place sugar and lemon juice in a saucepan and heat gently until sugar has dissolved, then boil rapidly for 1-2 minutes to the thread stage (when a little of the mixture placed between the backs of 2 teaspoons and pulled apart forms a thread). Pour the syrup in a steady stream onto the egg yolks, whisking all the time. Continue whisking until mixture is thick and pale. Beat the butter until light and fluffy, then gradually beat in the egg mixture, until thick.
5 Cut the cake into 2 layers. Sandwich together with lemon icing and cover the top and sides with more lemon icing. Pipe a border around the edge. Decorate with lemon shreds. **Serves 12**

CREAMY APRICOT ROLL

A naturally healthy filling of dried apricots blended with low fat soft cheese gives a fresh, fruity contrast to this light sponge roll. For a different flavour, try dried apples or peaches.

Swiss Roll:
3 eggs · 90g (3oz/1/3 cup) caster sugar · 90g (3oz/ 3/4 cup) plain flour

Apricot Filling:
125g (4oz/1 cup) pre-soaked dried apricots
185ml (6 fl oz/3/4 cup) orange juice
185g (6oz/3/4 cup) soft cheese

To Decorate:
icing sugar for dusting · 6 dried apricots, halved

1 First make the apricot filling: place the apricots and orange juice in a saucepan, bring to the boil, cover and cook gently until nearly all the juice is absorbed. Purée in a blender or food processor, then leave until cold. Place a third of the soft cheese in a piping bag fitted with a star nozzle and set aside. Beat the remainder into the apricot purée.
2 Lightly grease and line a 33 × 23cm (13 × 9 inch) Swiss roll tin. Preheat oven to 180C (350F/Gas 4).
3 Place the eggs and sugar in a heatproof bowl over a pan of simmering water and whisk until thick and pale. Remove bowl from saucepan and whisk until the mixture leaves a trail on the surface when the beaters are lifted.
4 Sift the flour onto the surface of the mixture and carefully fold in using a spatula until all flour is incorporated. Pour mixture into prepared tin and tilt tin from side to side to level the surface. Bake in oven for 10-15 minutes or until cake springs back when pressed in centre.
5 Turn cake out onto a piece of greaseproof paper dusted with icing sugar. Peel off lining paper, trim off edges and spread evenly with the apricot mixture. Roll up the sponge from the short edge. Cool on a wire rack. When cold, pipe with soft cheese and decorate with apricot halves. **Serves 10**

ST. CLEMENTS DRIZZLE CAKE

A delicious sponge cake – soaked in lemon syrup and topped with white chocolate and orange segments. As a variation, try a lemon flavoured sponge soaked in lime and covered with a dark chocolate topping.

1 orange · 2 lemons · 185g (6oz/1½ cups) self-raising flour · 185g (6oz/¾ cup) caster sugar · 185g (6oz) soft margarine · 3 eggs, beaten

Syrup:
125g (4oz/½ cup) caster sugar

Topping:
90g (3oz) white chocolate, melted
orange rind shreds

1 Lightly grease and line a 1kg (2lb) loaf tin. Preheat oven to 160C (325F/Gas 3).

2 Finely grate the rind from the orange and 1 lemon. Place in a bowl with the flour, sugar, margarine and eggs. Mix together with a wooden spoon, then beat for 1-2 minutes until light and fluffy.

3 Spoon the mixture into the prepared tin, smooth the top and bake for 1¼-1½ hours, or until the cake springs back when lightly pressed in the centre. Turn out onto a wire rack, remove paper and allow to cool.

4 To make the syrup, squeeze the juice from the lemons and place in a small pan with the sugar. Heat gently, stirring occasionally, until sugar has dissolved, then bring to the boil and boil for 15 seconds. Return cake to tin, pour over syrup and leave until cold.

5 Using a sharp knife, cut all of the white pith away from the orange and cut out the segments; dry on kitchen paper.

6 For the topping, pour the white chocolate along the top of the cake and arrange orange segments overlapping down the centre. Decorate with orange rind shreds. Leave until the chocolate is set. **Serves 12**

PINEAPPLE BALMORAL CAKE

A refreshing cake flavoured with the tang of fresh pineapple. Use canned pineapple as a standby.

1 small pineapple · 125g (4oz) butter, softened
125g (4oz/½ cup) caster sugar · 2 eggs, beaten
155g (5oz/1¼ cups) self-raising flour
30g (1oz/3 tablespoons) cornflour · 1 teaspoon baking powder

Pineapple Frosting:
120ml (4 fl oz/½ cup) pineapple (see right)
250g (8oz/1½ cups) icing sugar, sifted

To Decorate:
pineapple slices (see right)

1 Cut 3 thin slices from the pineapple and reserve for decoration. Peel remaining pineapple and cut out hard centre core. Finely chop 125g (4oz) pineapple. Purée the remaining pineapple in a blender or food processor; reserve for the frosting.

2 Grease and lightly flour a 30 × 10cm (12 × 4 inch) Balmoral cake tin. Preheat oven to 160C (325F/Gas 3). Beat the butter and sugar together in a bowl until light and fluffy. Gradually add the eggs, beating well after each addition. Sift flour, cornflour and baking powder over mixture and fold in carefully using a spatula until all flour is incorporated. Fold in chopped pineapple.

3 Place mixture in prepared tin, smooth top and bake for 55-60 minutes, or until cake springs back when pressed in the centre. Leave cake in tin for 5 minutes, then turn out onto a wire rack and leave until cold.

4 To make pineapple frosting, measure 120ml (4 fl oz/ ½ cup) pineapple purée and place in a bowl. Stir in icing sugar and beat until smooth. Pour frosting evenly over cake. Cut reserved pineapple slices into wedges and arrange on top of cake. Leave to set. **Serves 14-18**

NOTE: If you do not have a Balmoral cake tin, you can use a 1kg (2lb) loaf tin and allow an extra 10-15 minutes cooking.

CRANBERRY & CLEMENTINE CAKE

A cake with a festive feel, which can be made at any time with cranberries from the freezer.

185g (6oz/1 ½ cups) self-raising flour · 185g (6oz/ ¾ cup) caster sugar · 185g (6oz) butter, softened 3 eggs, beaten · 60g (2oz/¼ cup) cranberries, chopped

Frosting:
1 clementine · 185g (6oz/1 cup) icing sugar, sifted 90g (3oz) butter, softened

To Finish:
2 tablespoons boiling water · 1 tablespoon caster sugar · 8 cranberries

1 Lightly grease and line two 20cm (8 inch) round sandwich tins. Preheat oven to 160C (325F/Gas 3).
2 Mix together the flour, sugar, butter and eggs in a bowl, then beat with a wooden spoon for 1-2 minutes until smooth and glossy. Stir in the cranberries.
3 Divide mixture between prepared tins, smooth tops and bake in oven for 35-40 minutes, or until cakes spring back when lightly pressed in centre. Loosen edge with a palette knife, turn out onto a wire rack and leave until cold.
4 To make the frosting, set aside several thin strips of clementine peel. Grate remaining rind finely, squeeze 3 teaspoons juice and place in a bowl with the icing sugar and butter. Beat until light and fluffy. Place 4 tablespoons frosting in a piping bag fitted with a small star nozzle.
5 Sandwich cakes together with half the frosting and spread remainder over top. Pipe a frosting lattice and border on top of the cake.
6 Cut diamonds from the reserved clementine peel. Heat the water and sugar in a small saucepan, add the diamonds and simmer for 30 seconds, then remove with a fork. Add the remaining cranberries to the syrup and cook gently for 30 seconds. Leave until cold. Decorate the top of the cake with clementine diamonds and cranberries.

Serves 12

NECTARINE MELBA ROULADE

Impressive yet easy-to-make, this walnut sponge roll is filled with a creamy raspberry and nectarine filling and served with a fresh raspberry sauce. You can of course use peaches.

Roulade:

3 eggs, separated · 2 teaspoons water · 185g (6oz/ ¾ cup) caster sugar · 125g (4oz/1 cup) plain flour 60g (2oz/½ cup) ground walnuts

Filling and Decoration:

185g (6oz/¾ cup) soft cheese · 90ml (3 fl oz/ ⅓ cup) Greek yogurt · 3 nectarines, stoned and sliced · 375g (12oz/2 cups) raspberries 2 tablespoons icing sugar

1 Lightly grease and line a 33 × 23cm (13 × 9 inch) Swiss roll tin with non-stick baking paper. Preheat oven to 200C (400F/Gas 6).

2 Whisk the egg whites and water until stiff. Gradually add the sugar, whisking well after each addition, until the mixture stands in peaks. Beat the egg yolks in a separate bowl, then fold into meringue. Mix together the flour and nuts and carefully fold into the meringue.

3 Transfer mixture to prepared tin, level top and bake for 15-20 minutes, or until lightly browned and firm. Invert onto a piece of non-stick paper sprinkled with caster sugar. Trim off edges, then loosely roll up from a short edge, enclosing paper. Cool on wire rack.

4 To make the filling, beat together the soft cheese and yogurt; set aside 3 tablespoons for decoration. Reserve 8 nectarine slices for decoration, chop remainder and add to cheese mixture with 2 tablespoons raspberries. Mix lightly.

5 Carefully unroll cake and remove paper, spread filling evenly over and reroll firmly. Decorate with the piped cheese mixture, nectarine slices and 8 raspberries.

6 Sieve remaining raspberries into a bowl and stir in 1 tablespoon icing sugar. Dust roulade with remaining icing sugar and serve with raspberry sauce. **Serves 8**

CHEESECAKE GÂTEAU

A cheesecake with a difference – soft sponge and tangy fruity cheese layers. Other soft fruits can be used.

Sponge Base:

3 eggs · 90g (3oz/⅔ cup) caster sugar · 90g (3oz/¾ cup) plain flour

Filling:

185g (6oz/1½ cups) redcurrants · 185g (6oz/1½ cups) blackcurrants · 2 tablespoons caster sugar · 1½ packets lemon flavoured jelly 125g (4oz) unsalted butter · 250g (8oz/1 cup) soft cheese · 155ml (5 fl oz/⅔ cup) natural yogurt

To Finish:

155ml (5 fl oz/⅔ cup) whipping cream, whipped red and blackcurrants

1 Lightly grease and line a 33 × 23cm (13 × 9 inch) Swiss roll tin. Preheat oven to 180C (350F/Gas 4).

2 Place the eggs and sugar in a heatproof bowl over a pan of simmering water. Whisk until thick and pale. Remove bowl from pan and whisk until the mixture is thick enough to leave a trail on the surface when the beaters are lifted. Sift flour over mixture and fold in carefully. Pour mixture into prepared tin. Bake in oven for 10-15 minutes. Cool in tin.

3 Place fruit in separate pans; add 1 tablespoon water to each pan. Bring to boil, remove from heat and sieve into separate bowls; into each stir 1 tablespoon sugar.

4 Gently heat the jelly and butter in a saucepan until melted. Put the soft cheese, yogurt and jelly mixture into a food processor or blender and process until smooth. Divide between the fruit mixtures, stirring well. Leave until thickened.

5 Spread blackcurrant mixture over sponge base in tin; chill to set quickly. Spread redcurrant mixture on top and leave for several hours or overnight until set.

6 Carefully invert cake onto a baking sheet lined with non-stick paper. Peel off lining paper and turn cake right way up. Cut into three 10cm (4 inch) strips. Sandwich the layers together with cream. Decorate gâteau with piped cream and fresh fruit. **Serves 8**

FRANZIPAN FRUIT GÂTEAU

Layers of crisp light puff pastry filled with a moist almond filling and topped with a mixture of fresh fruits in season. Cut the pastry into any shape – square, round, oval or petal-shaped.

375g (12oz) puff pastry, thawed if frozen

Filling:

125g (4oz/1 ¼ cups) ground almonds · 125g (4oz/ ¾ cup) icing sugar, sifted · 1 teaspoon almond essence · 30g (1oz/¼ cup) plain flour · 125g (4oz) unsalted butter, softened · 2 eggs, beaten 250g (8oz/2 cups) mixed soft fruits, eg blueberries, raspberries, cherries, redcurrants

To Finish:

icing sugar for dusting

1 Cut pastry in half and roll out each piece on a lightly floured surface to a 25cm (10 inch) round. Place on a floured baking sheet and chill while making the filling.

2 Place the ground almonds, icing sugar, almond essence and flour in a bowl and stir well. In another bowl, beat the butter until soft, stir in the almond mixture and eggs, then beat until smooth.

3 Prick 1 pastry layer with a fork, spread almond filling over this layer to within 2.5cm (1 inch) of edge and cover with all but 2 tablespoons of the soft fruits. Dampen pastry edge, cover with remaining pastry round and seal edges well. Using a sharp knife, cut the pastry edge into scallops and mark fine lines on the top, radiating from the centre. Chill for 30 minutes before baking.

4 Preheat oven to 220C (425F/Gas 7). Bake pastry for 20 minutes, then reduce oven temperature to 200C (400F/Gas 6) and bake for a further 20 minutes or until the pastry is well risen and golden brown. Cool on a wire rack.

5 Dredge the top of the pastry with icing sugar and place under a hot grill to caramelize. Decorate the centre with the reserved soft fruits. **Serves 12**

HAZELNUT & REDCURRANT GÂTEAU

A melt-in-the-mouth meringue, richly flavoured with hazelnuts and filled with cream and redcurrants. Try any soft fruit in season, such as cherries, raspberries or strawberries, and flavour the meringue with lightly toasted walnuts, pine nuts or almonds.

Meringue:

185g (6oz/¾ cup) toasted hazelnuts, finely chopped · 1 teaspoon orange flower water ½ teaspoon cream of tartar · 1 teaspoon cornflour 4 egg whites · 250g (8oz/1 cup) caster sugar

Filling:

185g (6oz/½ cup) redcurrants · 185ml (6 fl oz/ ¾ cup) whipping cream, whipped

1 Lightly grease and base line two 20cm (8 inch) sandwich tins with non-stick baking paper. Sprinkle 2 teaspoons hazelnuts onto the sides of the tins and shake to coat evenly. Preheat oven to 180C (350F/Gas 4).

2 In a small bowl, mix together the orange flower water, cream of tartar and cornflour. Whisk the egg whites until stiff. Gradually add the sugar, whisking well after each addition. Whisk in the cornflour mixture until the meringue is stiff and glossy. Carefully fold in 125g (4oz/½ cup) hazelnuts, using a spatula, until evenly incorporated.

3 Divide mixture between prepared tins, smooth tops and bake in oven for 45-50 minutes until meringue is crisp and lightly browned on surface, but soft in centre. Cool in the tins. Carefully turn out meringues and remove paper.

4 To make filling, fold three quarters of the redcurrants into half of the cream and use to sandwich the meringue layers together. Cover the sides with a thin layer of cream and coat evenly with the remaining chopped hazelnuts. Put the remaining cream in a piping bag fitted with a star nozzle and pipe a ring in the middle and a shell border around the edge. Fill the centre with the remaining redcurrants. **Serves 10**

STRAWBERRY CREAM TORTE

Thin crispy layers filled with pastry cream and fruit make a light summer gâteau. Choose any fruits in season.

Torte:

2 egg whites · 125g (4oz/¾ cup) icing sugar, sifted 60g (2oz/½ cup) plain flour · 60g (2oz) unsalted butter, melted · 2 tablespoons chopped pine nuts 60g (2oz) chocolate, grated

Pastry Cream:

155ml (5 fl oz/⅔ cup) milk · 15g (½oz/ 6 teaspoons) plain flour · 2 teaspoons caster sugar 1 egg yolk · 1 teaspoon vanilla essence 155ml (5 fl oz/⅔ cup) double (thick) cream whipped

To Finish:

250g (8oz/1½ cups) strawberries, sliced icing sugar for dusting

1 Line 3 baking sheets with non-stick baking paper. Draw on three 18cm (7 inch) circles and eight 7.5cm (3 inch) circles. Preheat oven to 200C (400F/Gas 6).

2 Whisk the egg whites until very stiff. Gradually whisk in the icing sugar. Add the flour and butter; whisk until smooth. Spread a teaspoonful of mixture in each small circle. Spread remainder over large circles and sprinkle large circles with the nuts and half the grated chocolate.

3 Bake small circles for 5-8 minutes, remove with a palette knife and fold each into a cone shape. Wedge in a wire rack to cool. Cook large circles for 10-12 minutes. Cool on paper.

4 To make pastry cream, whisk 1 tablespoon milk with the flour, sugar, egg yolk and vanilla essence in a bowl. Bring remaining milk to the boil. Add to the flour mixture, whisking thoroughly. Return to the saucepan, bring to the boil and cook, stirring, for 1 minute. Leave until cold, then fold into the cream.

5 Set aside a quarter of the pastry cream. Add the rest of the chocolate and two thirds of the strawberry slices to remaining pastry cream and use to sandwich torte layers together. Pipe cones with pastry cream and arrange on torte. Dust with icing sugar and decorate with strawberry slices.

Serves 8

CANTELOUP GÂTEAU

Fragrant canteloup melon with crystallized ginger and lime makes this gâteau refreshingly different. Galia melon is equally good.

4 eggs · 125g (4oz/½ cup) caster sugar · 125g (4oz/1 cup) plain flour · 60g (2oz) unsalted butter, melted · finely grated rind of 1 lime

Filling:

315ml (10 fl oz/1¼ cups) double (thick) cream 4 tablespoons Greek yogurt · finely grated rind of 1 lime · 30g (1oz/¼ cup) crystallized ginger, chopped

To Decorate:

125g (4oz/¾ cup) pistachio nuts · 1 canteloup melon · crystallized ginger slices

1 Lightly grease, base line and flour a 23cm (9 inch) spring form cake tin. Preheat oven to 180C (350F/Gas 4).

2 Place the eggs and sugar in a heatproof bowl over a saucepan of simmering water and whisk until thick and pale. Remove bowl from saucepan and whisk until the mixture is thick enough to leave a trail on the surface when the beaters are lifted.

3 Sift the flour onto the mixture; add the butter and lime rind. Carefully fold in using a spatula until evenly incorporated. Pour mixture into prepared tin and bake for 35-40 minutes, until the cake springs back when lightly pressed in centre.

4 Loosen edges of cake with a knife, release tin and carefully turn cake out onto a wire rack. Leave until cold, then cut into 3 layers.

5 Whip cream and yogurt together until thick; reserve 6 tablespoons for piping. Set aside one third of remaining cream. Fold lime rind and ginger into the other two thirds; use to sandwich cake layers together. Cover top and sides with remaining cream. Reserve 12 pistachio nuts; chop remainder and use to coat sides of cake.

6 Cut the melon in half, scoop into small balls using a melon baller and arrange on top of gâteau. Pipe a cream border around the edge and decorate with crystallized ginger and pistachio nuts. **Serves 12**

CHERRY TOPPED MADEIRA

A good homely cherry madeira cake, with ground almonds added to keep the cake moist. Top with red and yellow glacé cherries and glacé fruits, or mixed dried fruits.

185g (6oz) butter, softened · 185g (6oz/¾ cup) caster sugar · 3 eggs, beaten · 185g (6oz/1½ cups) self-raising flour · 60g (2oz/½ cup) ground almonds 155g (4oz/¾ cup) glacé cherries, finely chopped

To Glaze:

2 tablespoons apricot jam · 2 teaspoons water 60g (2oz/⅓ cup) glacé cherries, halved · 3 glacé pineapple rings, cut into pieces

1 Lightly grease and line an 18cm (7 inch) round cake tin. Preheat oven to 160C (325F/Gas 3).

2 Beat the butter and sugar together in a bowl until light and fluffy. Gradually add the eggs, beating well after each addition. Sift in the flour, add the ground almonds and chopped cherries and fold carefully into mixture using a spatula.

3 Place mixture in prepared tin, smooth top and bake for 1 hour–1¼ hours or until cake springs back when pressed in the centre. Cool in tin for 5 minutes, turn out into a wire rack, remove the paper, invert cake and leave until cold.

4 For the glaze, place the apricot jam and water in a small pan and bring to the boil, stirring occasionally. Sieve and brush over top of cake. Arrange halved glacé cherries and pineapple pieces on top and brush with remaining glaze. Leave to set. **Serves 12**

SIMNEL CAKE

A traditional cake at Easter time. In my version tiny balls of marzipan are scattered throughout the moist, light fruit cake, instead of the usual solid marzipan layer.

375g (12oz/2 cups) mixed dried fruit · 50g (2oz/ ⅓ cup) glacé cherries · grated rind and juice of 1 small lemon · 185g (6oz) margarine · 185g (6oz/ 1 cup) light soft brown sugar · 250g (8oz/2 cups) self-raising wholewheat flour · 3 eggs, beaten · 375g (12oz) yellow marzipan

Topping:

2 tablespoons apricot jam, boiled and sieved 2 tablespoons icing sugar, sifted · 2 teaspoons lemon juice

To Decorate:

sugar-coated chocolate eggs

1 Lightly grease and line an 18cm (7 inch) round cake tin with greaseproof paper. Tie a double thickness band of brown paper around the outside of the tin and sit on a baking tray lined with a double thickness of brown paper. Preheat oven to 150C (300F/Gas 2).

2 In a bowl, mix together dried fruit, cherries, lemon rind and juice. Place the margarine, sugar, flour and eggs in a mixing bowl. Mix together with a wooden spoon, then beat for 1-2 minutes until smooth and glossy. Stir in the fruit.

3 Shape 125g (4 oz) marzipan into small balls. Spoon cake mixture into prepared tin and distribute the marzipan balls evenly throughout mixture. Smooth the surface. Bake in oven for 2½-2¾ hours, or until a warm skewer inserted into the centre of the cake comes out clean. Cool in tin. Turn out and remove paper.

4 Brush top of cake with apricot glaze. Shape 11 tiny marzipan eggs; roll remainder into an 18cm (7 inch) round and position on cake; flute the edge. Arrange marzipan eggs on top. Place under a preheated grill to brown lightly.

5 Mix the icing sugar with the lemon juice to make a smooth icing and spread in the centre of the cake. Arrange the sugar-coated eggs on top and leave to set. Finish with a yellow ribbon.

Serves 12

CHRISTMAS CAKE

A rich, easy-to-cut celebration fruit cake. Wrapped in foil, it will store in a cool place for up to 3 months. A week before Christmas, apply the marzipan and icing. Finish with a ribbon and simple decorations.

750g (1lb 8oz/4½ cups) mixed dried fruit · 125g (4oz/¾ cup) glacé cherries, chopped · 125g (4oz/1 cup) dried apricots, chopped · 90g (3oz/½ cup) stoned prunes, chopped · 60g (2oz/⅔ cup) brazil nuts, chopped · grated rind and juice of 1 lemon 3 tablespoons brandy · 280g (9oz/2¼ cups) plain flour · 2 teaspoons ground mixed spice · 220g (7oz) butter, softened · 60g (2oz/½ cup) ground almonds 220g (7oz/1⅓ cups) dark soft brown sugar 1½ tablespoons black treacle · 4 eggs, beaten

Icing and Decoration:

750g (1lb 8oz) white marzipan · 3 tablespoons apricot jam, boiled and sieved · 2 egg whites 2 teaspoons glycerine · 1 teaspoon lemon juice 500g (1lb/3 cups) icing sugar, sifted

1 Prepare a 20cm (8 inch) round cake tin as for Simnel Cake (page 231). Preheat oven to 140C (275F/Gas 1).
2 In a bowl, mix together the dried fruit, cherries, apricots, prunes, nuts, lemon rind, juice and brandy.
3 Mix the remaining cake ingredients together in a large bowl, then beat with a wooden spoon for 1-2 minutes until smooth and glossy. Add the fruit mixture and stir well.
4 Place the mixture in the prepared tin, smooth the top and bake in oven for 3-3¼ hours, or until a warm skewer inserted into centre of cake comes out clean. Cool in tin. Turn out, remove paper and place on a 25cm (10 inch) cake board.
5 Roll out the marzipan to a 25cm (10 inch) round. Brush the cake with apricot glaze, cover the top and sides with marzipan and trim to neaten. Allow to dry.
6 To make the icing, place the egg whites, glycerine and lemon juice in a bowl. Gradually beat in the icing sugar until the icing peaks softly. Spread evenly over the cake. Press a small palette knife onto the icing and pull away sharply to form peaks, leaving a smooth band around the side for a ribbon. Allow to dry.
7 When the icing has set, tie a ribbon around the cake and apply festive decorations. **Serves 24-30**

BIRTHDAY CAKE

A light, moist fruit cake suitable for icing or leaving plain. Once iced, it will keep for up to 3 months and may be decorated to suit any occasion. For the cake shown below you will need fresh flowers and about 2 metres of fancy ribbon.

500g (1lb/3 cups) mixed dried fruit · 125g (4oz/¾ cup) glacé cherries, chopped · 60g (2oz/½ cup) flaked almonds · grated rind and juice of 1 small orange · 375g (12oz/3 cups) plain flour · 1 teaspoon ground mixed spice · 280g (9oz/1½ cups) light soft brown sugar · 280g (9oz) butter, softened 4 eggs, beaten

Icing and Decoration:
750g (1lb 8oz) white marzipan · 3 tablespoons apricot jam, boiled and sieved · 750g (1lb 8oz) ready-to-roll icing · cornflour for dusting

1 Prepare an 18cm (7 inch) square cake tin as for Simnel Cake (page 231). Preheat oven to 140C (275F/Gas 1).
2 In a bowl, mix together the dried fruit, cherries, almonds, orange rind and juice. Place the remaining cake ingredients in another bowl, mix together with a wooden spoon, then beat for 1-2 minutes until smooth and glossy. Add the fruit mixture and stir well.
3 Place mixture in prepared tin, smooth top and bake in oven for 1¾-2 hours, or until a warm skewer inserted in the centre comes out clean. Cool in tin, turn out, remove paper and place on a 20cm (8 inch) square cake board.
4 Roll out the marzipan to a 23cm (10 inch) square. Brush cake with apricot glaze, cover with marzipan and trim off excess to neaten. Roll out the icing on a surface lightly sprinkled with cornflour to a 23cm (10 inch) square. Place on cake, smooth the top and sides, and trim off excess to neaten base.
5 Crimp the icing around the top and base of the cake using a small crimping tool dipped in cornflour. Tie a pretty ribbon around the side of the cake and arrange fresh flowers on top if you wish. **Serves 24-30**

DICE CAKES

Allow yourself a little extra time to ice these cakes – they are well worth the effort. I find it easier to place each cake on a large palette knife while applying the icing.

Sponge:
2 eggs · 60g (2oz/¼ cup) caster sugar · 60g (2oz/½ cup) plain flour · 30g (1oz) butter, melted

Icing and Decoration:
1 tablespoon apricot jam, warmed · 185g (6oz) marzipan · 375g (12oz/2¼ cups) icing sugar, sifted 3 tablespoons hot water · pink and yellow food colouring · 185g (6oz) small jelly sweets

1 Preheat the oven to 180C (350F/Gas 4). Grease and base line a 20cm (8 inch) square cake tin.

2 Place the eggs and sugar in a bowl over a pan of hot water. Whisk using an electric beater for about 10 minutes, until the mixture is light and thick enough to leave a trail when the beaters are lifted.

3 Sift the flour over the mixture and fold in carefully, using a metal spoon. Slowly pour the melted butter into the mixture and fold in. Pour into the prepared cake tin and gently shake the tin to level the mixture. Bake in the preheated oven for 20-25 minutes, until golden brown and firm to the touch. Leave in the tin for 5 minutes, then turn out and cool on a wire rack.

4 Brush the top of the cake with jam. Roll out marzipan to a 20cm (8 inch) square and use to cover the top of the cake. Cut the cake into 5 equal strips each way, to give 25 squares.

5 To make the icing, mix the icing sugar and water together until smooth and glossy. Transfer half the icing to another bowl. Colour one portion pink and the other yellow with a few drops of each food colouring. Coat half of the cakes with pink icing and half with yellow icing. Place on a wire rack and decorate with jelly sweets to resemble dice. Leave until the icing has set, then place in paper cake cases. **Makes 25**

SPIDER BUNS

Make these buns for your next Hallowe'en party, if not before!

Cake Mixture:
125g (4oz/1 cup) self-raising flour · 125g (4oz/ 1/2 cup) caster sugar · 125g (4oz) soft margarine 2 eggs · few drops of vanilla essence · 1 teaspoon baking powder

Icing and Decoration:
185g (6oz/1 cup) icing sugar, sifted 2 tablespoons hot water · 30g (1oz) plain (dark) chocolate · 1 packet chocolate buttons

1 Preheat the oven to 180C (350F/Gas 4).
2 Place all the cake ingredients in a mixing bowl and beat with a wooden spoon, or using an electric mixer, for 2-3 minutes until light and fluffy. Divide between 18 paper cake cases. Bake in the preheated oven for 12-15 minutes, until risen and golden brown. Transfer to a wire rack to cool.
3 To make the icing, mix together the icing sugar and water until smooth. Melt the chocolate in a bowl over hot water. Place the chocolate in a greaseproof paper piping bag and snip off the end (or use a small piping bag fitted with a fine nozzle). Place 1 tablespoon icing in a similar piping bag; set aside.
4 Spread the icing on top of the cakes and place a chocolate button in the centre of each one, for the spider. Use the melted chocolate to pipe 6 legs onto each spider. Use the reserved white icing to pipe on eyes. Leave until set. **Makes 18**

LION CAKE

Transform a basic sponge cake into a magical lion with the minimum of time and effort.
For the basic cake mixture, follow the recipe on page 235 replacing the vanilla essence with the grated orange rind.

3-egg basic cake mixture (page 235), flavoured with 1 teaspoon grated orange rind

Icing:
250g (8oz/1 ½ cups) icing sugar, sifted · 125g (4oz) soft margarine · 1 tablespoon orange juice · orange food colouring

To Finish:
30g (1 oz) plain (dark) chocolate · 2 white marshmallows · 2 blue sweets · 2 round wafer biscuits · 120g (4oz) box chocolate matchsticks

1 Preheat the oven to 160C (325F/Gas 3). Half-fill 2 paper cake cases with mixture, then turn the remainder into a greased and base lined 23cm (9 inch) round cake tin. Smooth the tops. Bake the small cakes for 10-12 minutes; the larger one for 30-35 minutes until golden brown and firm to the touch. Turn the large cake out and cool on a wire rack. Remove the paper cases.

2 To make the icing, mix the icing sugar, margarine and orange juice in a bowl and beat until light and fluffy. Add enough colouring to give a rich orange tone.

3 Split the large cake into 2 layers and sandwich together with a little of the icing. Place on a cake board, positioning the small cakes on either side for the ears. Trim the sides of the large cake to shape the face. Swirl the icing over the top and sides of the large cake, and on the top of the small cakes.

4 Using a piping bag fitted with a small plain tube, pipe a circle of chocolate for each eye, slightly larger than the marshmallows. Place the marshmallows on top and stick a sweet on each, using a little chocolate. Pipe chocolate in the centre of the ears, then pipe on eye-brows and nose. Position the biscuits as cheeks and pipe small chocolate dots on each.

5 Cut the chocolate matchsticks in half and place all around the lion's head for the mane. **Serves 12-15**

CLOWN CAKE

This appealing novelty cake is certain to delight young children and it is relatively simple to make. You will need 1 metre of wide spotted ribbon to make the large floppy bow. As a finishing touch, stick a few lollipops into the hat, but remember to have enough extra ones on hand for all the party guests!
For the basic cake mixture, follow the recipe on page 235.

3-egg basic cake mixture (page 235)

Filling and Decoration:
185g (6oz/½ cup) strawberry jam · 500g (1lb) ready-to-roll icing · yellow and red food colouring a little honey · 2 liquorice strips · 3 lollipops

1 Preheat oven to 160C (325F/Gas 3). Turn the cake mixture into a greased and base lined 23cm (9 inch) round cake tin; smooth top. Bake for 30-35 minutes, until golden brown. Turn out and cool on a wire rack.
2 Split the cake into 2 layers and sandwich together with two thirds of the jam. Place on a cake board and spread the remaining jam thinly over the top and sides.
3 Colour two thirds of the icing with a few drops of each colouring to give a flesh tone; knead until evenly coloured. Roll out and use to cover top and side of cake; trim off excess. Knead extra yellow colouring into trimmings to make orange icing. Wrap in plastic wrap.
4 Position a wide ribbon around the cake and tie with a bow. Colour half the remaining icing red. Shape a small piece into a ball for a nose; press onto cake. Divide remaining red icing in half. Shape one piece into a sausage 10cm (4 inches) long and flatten to form the hat brim. Form the other half into a D shape for the hat. Position the hat and brim on the cake.
5 Roll out orange trimmings and cut into thin strips for hair. Attach to cake on either side of hat. Roll out half the white icing to a sausage, 13cm (5 inches) long, flatten and curve on to the cake to form mouth. Shape remaining white icing into 2 deep eyes and position.
6 Trim eyes and mouth with liquorice, securing with a little honey if necessary. **Serves 12-15**

INDEX